BIBL

MW00638845

WHAT WE BELIEVE

AND

WHY WE BELIEVE IT

by
CHARLES F. BAKER

Published by

Grace Publications Inc.
2125 Martindale SW, Box 9432
Grand Rapids, Michigan 49509-0432

TABLE OF CONTENTS

AUTHOR'S PREFACE TO SECOND EDITION

The second edition of *Bible Truth* is issued with the fervent prayer that God will see fit to use it for the glory of Christ in helping to establish believers in what the Apostle Paul calls "my gospel, and the preaching of Jesus Christ, according to the revelation of the mystery, which was kept secret since the world began, but is now made manifest, and by prophetic scriptures, according to the commandment of the everlasting God, made known to all nations for the obedience of faith."

While printed originally to explain to other evangelical the doctrinal and dispensational position of the Grace Gospel Fellowship and related organizations, the volume has found considerable use as a basis for correspondence and Bible class courses, as it is actually a study of the outstanding doctrines of the Christian faith in the light of dispensational truth.

I have felt led to keep the Foreword just as Pastor O'Hair wrote it two years before his death, although as you read it you will recognize the fact that it was written in 1956 and that since that time *Milwaukee Bible College* has been moved to Grand Rapids, Michigan, where it operates under the name of *Grace Bible College*, and the name of *Worldwide Grace Testimony Mission* has been shortened to *Grace Ministries International.*

The only changes which have been made in the text are typographical corrections and the rewording of certain details of the doctrinal statement which has been done by the membership for purposes of clarification. These changes and additions have necessitated a difference in page numbering from the first edition.

FOREWORD

by Pastor J. C. O'Hair

During the past two or three generations there have been an increasing number of Bible teachers among Evangelical Christians, who have come out for the Premillennial coming of our Lord Jesus Christ. At some place and time along the way these "Premillennial 'grace' Bible teachers" picked up the name "Fundamentalists." Some of them prefer not to be called "Fundamentalists," but are willing to be called "Conservatives."

Many of the Premillennial Fundamentalists adopted the slogan,"The Book, The Blood, and The Blessed Hope." They have conscientiously, uncompromisingly and aggressively contended for the faith once for all delivered to the saints. "The Blessed Hope" in their slogan means that they contend for the premillennial coming of the Lord Jesus Christ (the Head) to rapture the members of His Body before He returns to earth, as the Son of man, to redeem His nation Israel and to establish on earth His prophesied "kingdom of heaven."

Of course all of us who are Evangelical Christians believe one hundred percent in the plenary inspiration of the Holy Scripture, in the eternal Deity of God the Father, God the Son and God the Holy Spirit. We believe in the Virgin Birth of our Lord and Saviour Jesus Christ, in His perfect, sinless life, and the Divine authority with which He spake as never man spake. We believe that by God's grace and power and by God-given faith in the Lord Jesus, the One Mediator between God and men, in His once-for-all prophesied sacrificial death and His bodily resurrection, any kind of sinner may be saved--eternally saved.

We believe that the Lord Jesus is now far above all heavens (Ephesians 4:8-11) on His Father's throne, *Head* of the *One Body*; that, in this age and dispensation of grace, every saved person is a member of that One Body, identified with Christ in His crucifixion, death, burial and resurrection. Moreover we believe that every such identified *Body-member* has been raised up and made to sit down in the heavenlies in Christ Jesus (Ephesians 2:4-6). This is one reason why we are uncompromisingly opposed to any and all "soul-sleeping" theories, the teaching of the unconscious state of either believer or unbeliever between death and resurrection. We are equally opposed to any and all *universal reconciliation* or *annihilation* teaching.

We believe that God's grace and power, which according to 2 Corinthians 9:8 and Ephesians 1:19-23 are available for every member of the Body of Christ, are altogether sufficient to enable every Body-member to know Christ in the fellowship of His suffering and in the power of His resurrection and to walk in the Spirit, well pleasing to God, as becometh a saint.

Premillennial *grace* Christians are, of course, dispensationalists, inasmuch as they believe that this present *grace* dispensation and the Church of this dispensation, which is the Body of Christ, began historically at the time of and because of the *fall* of Israel, and that Christ must and will come back to this earth, as the Son of man, before the beginning of the millennium, which will be after this present dispensation has suddenly ended by the rapture of the Church.

The great majority of these Premillennial *grace* dispensationalists teach dogmatically that the awful judgment of Christ upon Israel, recorded in the twenty-third of Matthew and ending with the pronouncement, "your house is left unto you desolate," is Scriptural proof that the *fall* of Israel took place before the Holy Spirit was poured out on the day of Pentecost. Humanly speaking, these "ACTS TWO" Premillenarians, who teach that this present dispensation and the *Joint-Body* of Ephesians 3:6 began historically with Peter and Pentecost, are in control of the Fundamentalists' Bible-schools and other organizations. They are united in their verdict that other Premillennial *grace* Bible-teachers, who hold that the *fall* of Israel and the historic beginning of the dispensation of grace and the *Joint-Body* was after Pentecost of Acts Two, are *ultradispensationalists.*

iv

Several years ago a number of Premillennial *grace* Bible teachers gathered together for Christian fellowship and Bible Study. They were convinced that the dispensation of the grace of God for Gentiles, called in Ephesians 3:9 "the dispensation of the mystery," did not begin either with Peter and Pentecost, or after the pronouncement of Acts 28:25-28 (which means after the period covered by the entire Book of Acts), but rather with the Apostle Paul before he wrote his first Epistle. They first of all saw the need for a missionary society to propagate this Gospel of the Grace of God in the regions beyond. The Worldwide Grace Testimony was organized for this purpose in 1939. Later in 1944 they decided to form an organization or fellowship to include Evangelical Christians who agreed with this dispensationalism. The name "GRACE GOSPEL FELLOWSHIP" was given to the organization. All of those who are identified with this Fellowship agree as touching the all-important fundamental doctrines of Evangelical Christianity, but they disagree with the type of dispensationalism that insists that this present grace dispensation and the Body of Christ began with Peter and Pentecost.

The need was soon felt for a Bible Institute where students, being trained for Christian work as evangelists, missionaries, pastors and teachers, should be taught to rightly divide the Word of Truth in obedience to
2 Timothy 2:15, to emphasize the difference between "the gospel of the kingdom" and "the gospel of the grace of God," to distinguish between the message and program of Peter and the Eleven in the first chapters of Acts and the Lord's spiritual message and program in "the dispensation of the mystery," revealed to and through the Apostle Paul. Therefore, in 1945, the officers and other members of the Grace Gospel Fellowship voted unanimously to establish THE MILWAUKEE BIBLE INSTITUTE (later The Milwaukee Bible College, and now Grace Bible College of Grand Rapids, Michigan).

By the unanimous vote of the members of the committee, chosen to purchase property and make the other necessary arrangements for the opening of the Institute, Mr. Charles F. Baker was elected President. Mr. Baker is a graduate of Wheaton College, also of Dallas Theological Seminary. He is a faithful, spiritual, able Bible expositor, well qualified for the duties of the office which he holds.

At the urgent request of the members of the official board of the College, and also by request of the directing officials of Grace Gospel Fellowship, president Baker wrote a series of articles for TRUTH magazine, published by the College, under the general heading, "What We Believe and Why We Believe It," setting forth what we believe doctrinally and dispensationally and what is taught the students who attend our College.

Now the directing officials of all three of the organizations mentioned above have decided to publish these monthly messages from the heart and pen of Mr. Baker in one volume. We are trusting and praying that the publication will fall into the hands of many sinners and saints, and that the saints, who read its messages, may be like the noble Bereans of Acts 17:11 and search the Scriptures to see if these things are so.

Mr. Baker was for a number of years a member of the church organization in Dallas, Texas, of which Dr. C. I. Scofield was the pastor. Dr. Scofield the author and editor of *The Scofield Reference Bible*, has caused Christians by the thousands to know the wisdom and importance of studying the Bible dispensationally. Several years after Dr. Scofield's Reference Bible had been published he gave his full and free and unqualified written endorsement to these printed statements: "In the latest Epistles of Paul it is noticeable that the *sign-gifts* (1 Corinthians 12:8-11) are nowhere in manifestation, but a *different order* is brought forth by the Holy Spirit for the correction of prevailing hobbies and fanaticisms"..."Is it the Spirit of God or Satan who turns the eyes of sincere Christians *back to Pentecost,* and away from the goal placed before them in Ephesians, Philippians and Colossians?" "There is a *corrective* passage in God's Word for every unbalanced position."

Being fully persuaded that today, as never before, a *corrective* dispensationalism is urgently needed, and that the Premillennial grace Bible teachers, who teach that "the dispensation of the mystery" and the "Joint Body" of Ephesians 3:6-11 began with Peter and Pentecost, do not offer the needed *corrective*, Mr. Baker's message is being sent forth in this volume, *What We Believe And Why We Believe It* with the sincere desire and hope that it may be read prayerfully by very many, with as little prejudice as possible.

INTRODUCTION

The basic beliefs of the Worldwide Grace Testimony (now Grace Ministries International) were set forth in a doctrinal statement at the time this mission society was organized. Later the Grace Gospel Fellowship and Milwaukee Bible Institute (now Grace Bible College) were organized and both adopted the same doctrinal platform.

A doctrinal statement is of necessity a very abbreviated and condensed statement of faith. While it serves its purpose well in identifying a movement relative to the truth of God's Word, it does need to be elucidated considerably in order to bring out some of the finer points of doctrine and to give sufficient Biblical evidence to convince others of its Scriptural character. It is merely a statement of what is believed without *the whys* and *the wherefores*. It shall be our purpose in what follows to endeavor to enlarge upon our bare statements of belief sufficiently to inform any interested person of the exact nature of our beliefs. It is to be hoped that this setting forth of our doctrine will not only be a blessing to those who are likeminded, but that our adverse critics, who often misrepresent our beliefs, will be considerate enough to carefully consider what is said here before attempting to inform others just what we do or do not believe.

The author is aware that no two men have ever seen eye to eye on every fine detail of truth. He is further aware that what he has written is primarily his own personal convictions about the truth, but he has conscientiously tried to write in a manner representative of the thinking of the *Grace Movement* as he has known it for the past twenty-five years. This material was published serially over the period of a year, and to the best of his knowledge no adverse criticisms were received from any of the members of the *Grace Gospel Fellowship.* A special word of thanks is due to Mr. C. R. Stam, editor of *The Berean Searchlight,* and to Pastor J. C. O'Hair of North Shore Church, Chicago, both of whom read the manuscript and offered helpful suggestions and criticisms.

THE BIBLE

IN KEEPING with all conservative, fundamental, orthodox believers we affirm the following concerning the Bible:

The entire Bible in its original writings is inerrant, being verbally inspired of God and is of plenary authority (2 Tim. 3:16,17; 2 Pet. 1:21).

This is practically the reiteration of Paul's statement: *"All Scripture is given by inspiration of God,"* or more literally, *is God-breathed.* We believe that the Bible is completely and entirely divine, that it is indeed and in truth the Word of God. At the same time we believe that it is also entirely human, in the sense that every word of it was written down by men, as Peter states in the passage referred to above. It is perfectly human and perfectly divine, even as our blessed Lord Jesus Christ is.

We reject unreservedly all the theories of the school of the destructive higher critics which would either place a much later date upon the various Bible books than their internal evidence would naturally indicate, or which would deny the stated authorship of these books. Any such teaching must effectually deny the unique inspiration which the Bible claims for itself.

But not only is the entire Bible divinely inspired in its original writings; it is all profitable. It is most important to stress this point, especially in view of the further fact that the Bible came into being as a progressive revelation from God. The Bible is a dispensational book. It is patent upon the surface of many passages that not all of the Bible is addressed to nor is written about the same group of people. Surely none of the New Testament epistles were written to people who lived before the coming of Christ, and it is just as evident that the Old Testament books were not addressed to those who live under this present dispensation. Upon the basis of this fact some would suppose therefore that those parts of the Bible which were not written to us must be discarded, and in fact this charge has often been made against those who recognize the

1

dispensational character of the Bible. Some have gone so far as to accuse the dispensationalist of destroying the Bible as effectively as does the modernist, only using another method. It has even been claimed that dispensationalism is far worse than open infidelity, because it begins by piously affirming the divine inspiration of the Bible but ends by cutting it to pieces. Thus sincere people are seduced by this teaching, only to find in the end that they do not have any Bible left.

We would be as quick as any to denounce any system which would discard any portion of the Bible. We believe that the wonderful, divine character of the Bible is seen in the fact that while its various parts were written over many centuries and to peoples under different dispensations of God's government, it is ALL profitable for us today. Only a divinely inspired book could possess such a character. The Scripture itself is clear on this point: it is *"profitable for doctrine, for reproof, for correction, for instruction in righteousness; that the man of God may be perfect, thoroughly furnished unto all good works."*

Must Be Rightly Divided

The apostle Paul, to whom was committed the dispensation of the mystery and in whose epistles alone we find this distinctive revelation, tells us that all that was written aforetime is for our admonition, and is therefore profitable to us (1 Cor. 10:11). Anyone who divides the Word in order to discard parts of it does greatly err, not knowing the truth, and manifestly does not *rightly* divide the Word of truth.

Apart from right division of the Scripture, however, one is bound to get into hopeless confusion. Almost all Christians recognize the necessity of dividing between the Old and New Testaments. Who would contend that the commands in the law of Moses concerning the offering of animal sacrifices or practicing of circumcision were binding upon believers today? Some would tell us that these Old Testament commands have been superseded by new ones and that we today are only under obligation to obey all of the commands in the New Testament. But we would ask, Just what is the New Testament?

In the four Gospels and in the book of Acts which are included in the twenty-seven books which make up the so-called New Testament, we find many commands and practices which these same people do not obey any more than they do those of the Old Testament. To sell all and to have all things common, to obey those that sit in Moses' seat, to go forth preaching without gold or silver or even such provision as a change of raiment, to kill and eat the Passover lamb, to heal the sick, cleanse the lepers, cast out demons, and raise the dead--all of these are commands and practices contained in the book which we call the New Testament.

Distinctions Must Be Made

It is evident in the light of the above statements and of dozens of similar ones that in order to rightly divide the Word we must recognize other distinctions than the two main divisions of our Bible. Anyone who carefully approaches the study of the Bible must acknowledge that the Old Testament did not begin until Moses, some fifteen hundred years before Christ and at least twenty-five hundred years after Adam. Therefore Genesis actually contains none of the Old Testament. Likewise it must be acknowledged that the New Testament was made in the blood of Christ so that the bulk of the four Gospels are not yet upon New Testament ground.

We contend, however, that even this further distinction is not sufficient for rightly dividing the Word of truth. The book of Acts is surely upon New Testament ground, as it follows the death and resurrection of Christ, but it also contains much that is not practiced and preached by evangelical Christians today. Tongues, healings, miracles, raising the dead, water baptism for the remission of sins, having all things common, and even a preaching to none but unto the Jews only, are all a part and parcel of the early half of that book. It is true that Pentecostal people today tarry and seek and strive to duplicate these miraculous manifestations, with results that are evidently dubious; but why do not the bulk of evangelicals include these things in their religious and spiritual program, if they belong to the so-called New Testament?

Distinctive Truth of the Mystery

The only division of the Scripture which meets all conditions and harmonizes the entire Bible is one that takes into account the distinctive revelation of the dispensation of the mystery. The New Covenant as such was prophesied in Jer. 31:31 and is a part of that divine undertaking which will be consummated when Jesus Christ is reigning as King of

3

Israel and King of kings here upon the earth. All of the Old Testament is prophetic of that glorious kingdom. The four Gospels present that kingdom as at hand. The early part of the Acts shows the necessity of the sufferings of Christ and the bringing in of the New Covenant before that kingdom could be established, and further offers that kingdom to Israel upon the condition of national repentance. But the book of Acts is also a record of Israel's final rejection of the Messiah and His kingdom, and of God's raising up and sending forth of a new apostle with a new and distinctive dispensation. Paul's epistles contain that new revelation from the ascended and glorified Christ. That revelation is designated as the Mystery which was never before made known to the sons of men in other ages and generations.

Therefore, it is unique and distinct from that great body of truth which will see its consummation in the Millennial earth. We believe with Dr. C. I. Scofield that in Paul's writings alone "*we find the doctrine, position, walk, and destiny of the church*" of this dispensation (p. 1252 Scofield Reference Bible). This means that Paul's epistles contain the specific instructions for believers today. Of course, there is much in common with these instructions throughout the entire Bible.

To summarize: we believe that the entire Bible is verbally inspired in its original writings, that it is in its entirety profitable for us today, but not that it is in its every part profitable for the same thing. We believe that for an intelligent understanding of the Bible we need to follow the divine injunction to rightly divide it. We believe that in order to do this we must not only recognize the several dispensations under which God placed His people Israel in reference to the earthly, Messianic kingdom, but we must clearly distinguish all of this from God's present "mystery" purpose with the Body of Christ. We further believe that the entire Pauline revelation is one complete revelation of truth for members of the Body of Christ. We deny what some extreme dispensationalists affirm, that Paul's earlier epistles are not addressed to members of the Body of Christ in this dispensation. We believe that any confession to belief in the divine inspiration of the Bible which does not recognize these divine distinctions is bound to result in the confusion of the believer today in his understanding of God's will, in his practice, and in his message.

We further believe that the Bible is of plenary authority; that is, that its authority in matters of our faith and practice is full and complete. It is the supreme court to which we must bring all questions of faith and morals for final decision. Church history, church councils, creeds and the like may contain much truth, but these things are in no sense the basis for authority of what is truth. "Thy Word is Truth."

THE GODHEAD

VERY briefly stated, all of those who are associated with the Grace Gospel Fellowship believe that " **there is ONE God, eternally existing in three Persons: Father, Son ant Holy Spirit. Deut. 6:4; 1 Tim. 2:5; Eph. 4:4- 6; Matt. 28:l9; 2 Cor. 13:14.**" We must emphasize this fact, for there are some who hold to a dispensational interpretation of the Scripture who are Unitarian as concerns the Godhead. All such deny the deity of our Lord Jesus Christ and the personality of the blessed Holy Spirit. Satan has used such people to frighten sincere saints of God from studying or accepting dispensational truth, making them believe that there is some subtle connection between dispensationalism and a denial of the Trinity, and that if one accepts dispensational truth he must logically end up in denying the deity of Christ.

Actually, of course, there is not the slightest connection between dispensational truth and Unitarianism. In the long history of Unitarianism from Arius in A. D. 325 to the present, no case can be found where dispensational truth led anyone into this heresy. As a matter of fact, it can be seriously doubted whether any Unitarian up to the present day "Concordant Version Movement" even recognized that there was such a thing as dispensational truth. Satan knows well that God's distinctive message of grace for this present dispensation can only be known through means of the dispensational interpretation of the Word, and he has seen to it that wherever an attempt has been made to recover this precious truth his emissaries have crept in with some damnable heresy to contaminate the message, and thus to confuse the minds of sincere believers and to turn them against the only thing that can bring them into the fullness of understanding of the mystery of Christ.

Since no one who professes to be a theist denies the deity of God the Father, we will not take space to set forth this truth, other than to point out the obvious fact that if God the Father is eternal, then there must of necessity have been an eternal Son to maintain that eternal relationship. God the Father is first and foremost the God and Father of our Lord Jesus Christ (Eph. 1:3; Col. 1:3; 2 Cor. 1:3; 1 Peter 1:3). After that He is the Father of all who believe on the Lord Jesus Christ (Gal 3:26; Rom. 1:7; 8:15; 2 Cor. 1:2; Eph. 1:2). While God is presented as the Creator of all, He is never referred to in Scripture as the Father of all men. Since the fall of man, or at least since the coming of Christ into the world, all unsaved men are represented as having Satan as their father (John 8:42-44; Eph. 2:2; 5:6; Col. 3:6). If there were such a thing as the universal Fatherhood of God there would be no place left for the doctrine of the new birth.

We believe that the Scriptures clearly teach the perfect humanity and the perfect deity of our Lord Jesus Christ. The doctrine of the Godhead may be inscrutable to the finite mind, but what truth even in nature about us is not also ultimately beyond the power of the human mind to grasp? A college science textbook, published in 1953, in trying to describe an electron states: "*From each experiment we try to make ourselves a picture, a mechanical model in ordinary terms, which will help us understand how electrons behave. But have we any assurance that a model based on ordinary experience can be applied to particles less than a thousand billionth of a centimeter in diameter? Isn't it conceivable that the electron is something impossible to picture with everyday concepts, something which in one experiment may act as a particle and in another as a wave? . . . The question we posed at the beginning of this section, 'Is the electron a wave or a particle?' is meaningless in the sense that no experiment can be devised to give us the answer" (Fundamentals* of *Physical Science*, by Krauskopf, pp. 328, 329). If it is true that the infinitesimal defies our powers of definition and description, is it not evident that the Infinite must likewise do the same? Just because we cannot conceive how the Father, the Son and the Holy Spirit can be one God, is no more reason to reject this truth of God's revelation than it is to reject the revelation of nature that light and electrons exhibit characteristics of both particles and waves, a seeming contradiction.

There can be no doubt that the Scriptures bear abundant proof that there is but one God (Dent. 6:4; Isa. 44:6-8; 1 Tim 2:5; 1 Cor. 8:4). Likewise, there can be no doubt that the Scriptures speak of three as being God. The Father is called God in Rom. 1:7; the Son is called God in Heb. 1:8; John 1:1; Rom. 9:5; 1 John 5:20; Titus 2:13; the Holy Spirit is called God in Acts 5:3,4. These three---Father, Son and Holy Spirit---are not merely three modes or offices in which God has manifested Himself at different times, as Sabellius taught, but they are three distinct Persons, often mentioned together, as in Matt. 28:19, where we read, "in the name [not names] of the Father, and of the Son, and of the Holy Ghost." Paul is fond of bringing these Persons together in his epistles, as he does in his benediction in 2 Cor. 13:14: "The grace of our Lord Jesus Christ, and the love of God, and the communion of the Holy Ghost be with you all."

7

All attempts to rationalize the doctrine of the Trinity have failed. Nathan R. Wood, in his book, *The Secret of the Universe*, has brought some very helpful facts to light however, in showing that the creation reveals in many ways the character of its Creator. Simply stated, he shows that there are just three basic elements which comprise the Universe: space, matter and time. Each of these manifests a remarkable triunity. All of space is included in length, breadth and height. Space has absolute threeness. Apart from any one of these dimensions space would cease to exist. Yet space is genuinely one, having the same kind of oneness as we find in the Trinity. All of space is length; all of it is height; all of it is breadth. Each dimension is the whole of space. So in the Trinity, each person is the whole of God, not just a part of God. The same kind of three-foldness can be seen in matter and in time. These things are not illustrations of the Trinity, but rather serve to show how the Trinity of the Godhead has been manifested in the works of creation.

The Godhead and Christ

As Christians, and especially as exponents of Pauline theology, the most fundamental and underlying doctrine is that of the deity of Christ. We believe that **"Jesus Christ was begotten by the Holy Spirit and born of the Virgin Mary and is true God and true man (Luke 1:35; Phil. 2:6-9 Rom. 1:3,4)."** The difficulty of comprehending this doctrine seems to inhere in the title, *"the only begotten Son."* If He is a begotten Son, how can He be eternal? We have already seen that the Father can be no more eternal than the Son, but here it is important to understand that the terms *only begotten* and *first begotten* do not necessarily have to do with generation in time, but are titles of privilege. When Col. l:l5 states that He is the firstborn of all creation, it does not mean that He was the first creature to be born; for the next verses plainly tell us that He existed before all created things, and that He Himself created everything that was created, which would necessarily exclude Himself. The firstborn in the Scripture is the title of inheritance and of headship. It is just another way of saying that Christ is the heir of all things (Heb. 1:2). In this connection, Ps. 89:27 is most enlightening. God speaking in this Messianic psalm says: *"Also l will make him my firstborn, higher than the kings of the earth."*

The Pauline doctrine of salvation demands a divine Savior. The doctrine of a merely good man being made sin for all mankind, of God punishing a good man in the place of the guilty, is at once unethical and abhorrent.

8

The modernist, after denying the deity of Christ, is right in denouncing the Pauline doctrine of salvation as unethical. But the modernist is wrong about the deity of Christ, and therefore wrong in denouncing Christ's death as a substitutionary sacrifice for us. The One who died on Calvary's cross was not only a man; He was God manifested in the flesh. He was the very One we had all sinned against, who took our place. There can be no objection from the ethical standpoint to God Himself paying our debt, bearing our sin; and that is exactly what He did in the person of Jesus Christ.

There is one verse of Scripture, Heb. 13:8, which at once proves the deity of Jesus Christ and also suggests the dispensational aspects of the Incarnation: "*Jesus Christ, the same yesterday, and today and for ever.*" This One was none other than the God unto whom the Psalmist cried: "*But thou art the same, and thy years shall have no end*" (Ps. 102: 27). He is the unchanging One, and yet He has changed. He surely changed His form; for He had subsisted eternally in the form of God, but in time He changed His form and was made in the form of man (Phil. 2:6-8). He lived on earth for some thirty-three years in a body of flesh and blood, and then died that He might reconcile the world unto God. Death and resurrection brought another change, and now, although we have known Christ after the flesh, yet henceforth know we Him so no more (2 Cor. 5:16). He presented Himself while on earth as the King of Israel. Now at the right hand of God He has become Head over all things to the church which is His Body (Eph. 1:22, 23). He is unchanging in His essential deity, but in His humanity and in His dispensational relationships with Israel and the Body we must surely recognize the great changes which have taken place. It is our great desire and burden to help believers see these changes and distinctions, in order that they might the better understand what is the hope of His calling, and what are the riches of the glory of His inheritance in the saints, and what is the exceeding greatness of His power to usward who believe.

TOTAL DEPRAVITY

IN COMMON with most Fundamentalists we believe in the total depravity of the natural man. **"All men by nature are dead in trespasses and sins and are, therefore, totally unable to do anything pleasing to God (Eph. 2:1- 3; Rom. 3:9-12)."**

The doctrine of total depravity could hardly be considered a dispensational one, since man has been in this condition ever since the fall in Eden, but a careful study of the Scripture will show that this doctrine comes into full manifestation in the divine revelation which was given to the Apostle Paul for this dispensation of the grace of God. In fact, it should be apparent to any thoughtful student of the Word that the full blaze of the glory of the grace of God could only be displayed upon the foil of man's completely helpless and hopeless condition. Therefore it will be observed that the more Pauline a man is in his theology the more he will contend for this truth. On the other hand, one who opposes the teaching of man's natural total depravity can be counted upon to be anti-Pauline also. There are many who profess to believe in man's depravity who practically deny the fact by their preaching of human works as a factor in salvation.

Human or Divine Standards?

By stating that the natural man is totally depraved we do not mean that every man is a slave to every known sin, or that by practice he is the worst sinner possible, or that he is destitute of conscience, or that he has no ability to do that which is useful and pleasing to man when judged by human standards. It is manifestly evident from everyday observation that unsaved people are capable of many acts of decency and honesty, of philanthropy and good will. While much of this milk of human kindness is seen only in environments which have a Christian background, it nevertheless remains true that many unsaved people possess likeable and pleasing traits of character. The natural man is capable of being highly religious, of curtailing his fleshy appetites, and even of so closely imitating the Christian life as to deceive the most discerning. If then it is possible for a non-Christian to live a better outwardly moral life than some Christians live, where is the place for talking about total depravity, and wherein lies the boasted supremacy of the Christian life?

In answer to the latter question it should be pointed out that the Christian possesses both his old depraved nature and the new nature. The old is still capable of manifesting itself and will inevitably manifest itself unless the Christian is living in the conscious power of the indwelling Spirit of God and in the victory which is his over sin through co-crucifixion with Christ.

In answer to the former question it needs to be stated that Christianity is not merely morality. It is, of course, the most highly moral and ethical of all systems known to man---but it is more than that. Christianity is life toward God. It is that which overcomes all enmity toward God, which removes every barrier that stands between God and man, and which perfectly reconciles man unto God so that his life and actions may be pleasing and acceptable to God.

In other words, the natural man is just the opposite of what has been stated above. He has no life toward God; he is dead through his trespasses and sins; he is at enmity against God; he is alienated from the life of God; he is incapable of pleasing God by anything that he may strive to do. These statements are based upon the clear facts of divine revelation. The natural man is totally destitute of love to God, so that no thought, act or emotion can be acceptable to God. He is supremely determined by a preference of self to God. He is incapable by any act of his will to bring his life and character into conformity to God's holy standard.

Depravity Produces Self-righteousness

When one takes the mask from all of the religions in the world it is seen that they all have one thing in common with the Jews' religion of Paul's day: "*For they being ignorant of God's righteousness, and going about to establish their own righteousness, have not submitted themselves unto the righteousness of God*" (Romans 10:3). Self-righteousness is the product of man's depraved nature. The righteousness of God is God's gift to the sinner who believes the Gospel that Christ died for his sins. Even Isaiah of old got a glimpse of Christ in His glory (John 12:41) and realized that the very best of man's self-righteousness was but filthy rags in the sight of God (Isa.. 64:6). Paul confessed that in his flesh there dwelt no good thing (Romans 7:18). *"The Lord looked down from heaven upon the children of men to see if there were any that did understand, and seek God. They are all gone aside, they are all together become filthy: there is none tat doeth good, no, not one"* (Ps. 14:2,3).

11

Depravity Is Enmity toward God

Man's depravity then consists in the settled state of his will. We might say that as far as God is concerned man's will is a won't. All of the good deeds and religious acts that the natural man does are motivated not by love to God, but by self-love. He may give millions to charity; he may go on long and laborious religious pilgrimages, but his motive is not love for God, but a desire to make a fair show in the flesh (Gal. 6:12), or to be seen and honored of men (Matt 6:1), or perhaps to try to pay for his own sins and thus benefit himself in the life to come. God looks on the heart and not on the outward appearance (1 Sam. 16:7).

Many of those who profess to believe that the fall brought about a state of total depravity have modified the doctrine in various ways by supposing that God gave to all mankind after the fall a kind of common grace or ability to do good, so that, in fact, this natural depravity is overcome. This teaching, while finding no direct support in the Scripture, appears to be essential in the thinking of those who practically deny the sovereignty of God and His election and magnify the free will of man. If man is still totally depraved, how, they reason, could anyone turn to God and be saved? Therefore if there is a "whosoever gospel," there must be an enabling given to all mankind to make it possible for them to turn to God. All such schemes are designed to try to get God out of a dilemma in which He appears to be unrighteous and partial. They all end up, however, in another dilemma, and in doing violence to the plain teaching of the Scripture. If God gives the same enabling power to all men to be saved, why are not all saved? If God has no elective choice, it must be because some are naturally better and more God-like than others. In the final analysis, then, all who get saved can boast that they got saved, partly by the enabling grace of God and partly by some inherent goodness. But this is a plain denial of Scripture, and it is also a denial of the original tenet that man was totally depraved by the fall before the common grace was given; for where did this inherent goodness come from that makes some better than others? No, none of these schemes explain; they only serve to exalt man and to belittle the grace of God.

Depravity, Election and Responsibility

It is not in order to elucidate upon the doctrine of election at this point, but it should be stated that man's inability to please God is not a physical inability, but a moral and spiritual one. A man who is a sworn enemy of another man surely is not physically incapacitated as far as doing good to his enemy is concerned. He could do good if he would, just the same as he does to his friends. But he does not and cannot do good toward his enemy because of the enmity that exists. Just so, *"the carnal mind is enmity against God: for it is not subject to the law of God, neither indeed can be. So then they that are in the flesh cannot please Gods* (Romans 8:7,8). This spiritual inability or depravity then, instead of providing an excuse for man to claim that he is not responsible and that he could not be saved if he wanted to, is actually a cause of his condemnation. He could believe the Gospel if he wanted to, but he does not want to because of his enmity toward God. The fact that man can believe the devil's lie is proof that he possesses the power of faith. It is because he is wrong at heart and guilty; because he has a depraved nature for which he is responsible that God can and will hold every man accountable for not accepting the Gospel.

Under such circumstances no man could ever be saved apart from a special working of God, call it what we will. The Scripture says: *"whom he did foreknow, he also did predestinate . . . whom he did predestinate, them he also called; and whom he called, them he also justified: and whom he justified, them he also glorified* (Rom. 8:29,30). Foreknowledge is not God knowing beforehand which people would have the inherent goodness which would cause them to believe, for we have already seen that any such idea is contradictory to the Scripture. God's foreknowledge includes all of God's omniscience based upon His holy plans and purposes. On the basis of this entire and infinite foreknowledge of all things possible and actual, we believe that God chose that which He saw to be the best, and although not understandable to us because we do not possess this infinite foreknowledge, some are going to be lost and some saved. Those who are lost will be held entirely responsible for their lost condition, and those who are saved will owe their salvation entirely to the free grace of God.

Depravity Emphasized under Grace

Before concluding this chapter in *What We Believe*, we should notice that the doctrine of total depravity finds its full manifestation in the revelation given to Paul, just as does the truth of the grace of God. In Old Testament times God had a chosen nation. He set them apart from all other nations.

13

They were near to God by reason of the covenants (Eph. 2:12,17), while the Gentiles were afar off. Under such circumstances it would be difficult to lump all mankind together and say that there was no difference. Jesus referred to the Israelites as children and to the Gentiles as dogs (Matt. 15:26). There is surely a great difference between the character of children and dogs. The same relationship is still recognized by Peter after Pentecost in Acts 3:25, as far as Israel is concerned.

After Israel's fall, however, and the setting aside temporarily of the covenants of promise, we see in Paul's epistles how he goes back beyond David and Abraham, all the way to Adam, and shows that all mankind, Jews and Gentiles alike, share in the alienation which Adam brought upon the race, and that all are by nature children of wrath. Now it can truly be said that there is no difference between Jew and Gentile. Of course, all along the Jew had a fallen nature, but he had been in a special place of privilege. Now the privilege is past and the Jew finds himself to be but a son of fallen Adam, just as depraved as the Gentile.

Of necessity God must bring the whole of mankind to this place before He could make known the ministry of reconciliation and the riches of His grace. These truths are the distinctive factors in the special revelation vouchsafed to the Apostle Paul. He it is who informs us that the casting away of Israel has resulted in the reconciling of the world (Rom. 11:15), so that the reconciliation could not have been manifested so long as Israel stood in covenant privilege. He it is who shows us that there is no difference between Jew and Gentile, either as to nature or as to the way of salvation (Rom. 3:23; 10:2; Eph. 2:3,14,15). He it is who tells us that this present dispensation is the dispensation of the grace of God and the dispensation of the mystery (Eph. 3:2-9; Col. 1:25-27).

Therefore we contend earnestly for the distinctive truth of the Pauline revelation. We see that it bears an important influence upon every doctrine of our Christian faith. We view with dismay all of the confusion and wreckage which have been caused by a neglect or a refusal of Pauline truth. We understand why it is that the natural man hates as he hates nothing else the doctrine of God's unmerited grace with its corollary doctrine of man's total depravity. We marvel at that same grace which in God's own mysterious working brought us to see our hopeless condition and wrought in us that work of regeneration which imparted to us a new nature and granted to us the indwelling of His Holy Spirit, who also

14

baptized us into the body of Christ. Truly, Christ's special and unique revelation for mankind today is that which He gave from heaven after His ascension to the Apostle of the Gentiles.

REDEMPTION

IN OUR doctrinal statement, the word *Redemption* is used to cover the whole of God's saving work. **"God justifies ungodly sinners by His grace, upon the ground of the blood of Christ, through the means of faith. This complete salvation is bestowed as the free gift of God apart from man's works (Rom. 3: 24-28; 5:1,9; Eph 2:8,9)."**

Without doubt the great majority of the millions of adherents to the various denominations and sects of Christendom believe something about redemption or salvation. They all believe that something was accomplished by Christ to make possible the salvation of mankind. But there is almost endless disagreement and confusion on the subject of just what He accomplished for us, and of how we receive the benefits of His accomplishments Therefore we will consider first the Provision of Salvation, and then the Application of Salvation.

The Provision of Salvation

In our last chapter on the Total Depravity of Mankind, we saw the absolute need of salvation and the complete inability of man to provide it. Therefore the provision must come entirely apart from mankind, which is equivalent to saying that it must come from God. This fact is echoed in dozens of familiar Scripture phrases----*"the salvation of the Lord," "the horn of my salvation," "O God of our salvation," "Salvation belongeth unto the Lord," "thou art the God of my salvation," "Neither is there salvation in any other," "the salvation of God is sent unto the Gentiles," "the power of God unto salvation to every one that believeth," "of salvation, and that of God," "the grace of God that bringeth salvation."*

Dispensational Considerations

The doctrine of Salvation, like other doctrines, must be studied dispensationally. Salvation to the Old Testament saints included God's deliverance from physical enemies. Over and over again the people of Israel were reminded of their redemption out of Egypt (Ex. 15:13; Deut. 7:8; 9:26; 13:5,10; 1 Chron. 17:21, etc.). This aspect of redemption is perfectly legitimate, not only in reference to Old Testament Israel, but to New Testament Israel as well. Zacharias, the father of John the Baptist,

16

filled with the Holy Spirit, uttered these words in Luke 1:68-75: *"Blessed be the Lord God of Israel; for he hath visited and redeemed his people, and hath raised up an horn of salvation for us in the house of his servant David; as he spoke by the mouth of his holy prophets, which have been since the world began: that we should be saved from our enemies, and from the hand of all that hate us; to perform the mercy promised to our fathers, and to remember his holy covenant; the oath which he swore to our father Abraham, that he would grant unto us, that we being delivered out of the hand of our enemies might serve him without fear, in holiness and righteousness before him, all the days of our life."*

These divinely-inspired words, which encompass all of Israel's covenants and promises and all of the writings of the prophets since the world began, are sufficient evidence that redemption and salvation include, besides the forgiveness of sins, the idea of national deliverance from all enemies in the Messiah's earthly kingdom.

It should also be noted that, in the shadow days of the Old Covenant, redemption was by money---*"Moses took the redemption money of them"* (Num. 3:49). This is doubtless for the purpose of showing us that redemption does involve the idea of paying a ransom price. However, Peter, writing to the elect of Israel in the dispersion, makes it plain that money could not actually redeem, but was only typical of the blood of Christ: *"Forasmuch as ye know that ye were not redeemed with corruptible things, as silver and gold, from your vain conversation received by tradition from your fathers; but with the precious blood of Christ...."*
(1 Pet. 1:18,19). The book of Hebrews also makes it very plain: *"Neither by the blood of goats and calves, but by his own blood he entered in once into the holy place, having obtained eternal redemption for us"* (Heb. 9:12). Paul in writing to members of the Body of Christ shows us that the same truth applies to us today: *"In whom we have redemption through his blood, the forgiveness of sins, according to the riches of his grace"* (Eph. 1:7, cf. Col. 1:14).

Through, or in Spite of Israel?

While redemption and salvation have reference only to Israel in Old Testament times and even while Christ was on earth, the distinction is not that redemption refers only to Israel and not to the Gentiles under the kingdom program. To begin with it did include only Israel, but it was intended ultimately for all of the world *through Israel.* Israel must first be filled before the blessing could go to the Gentiles. But in this present dispensation of the mystery, salvation has been sent to the Gentiles in spite of Israel and to provoke Israel to jealousy. Further distinctions are that dispensationally in Old Testament times redemption was by money and by animal blood, but from the death of Christ onward, whether in the dispensation of the kingdom or of the grace of God, it is by the precious blood of Christ and that redemption under the kingdom program, whether past or future involves national deliverance of Israel from all enemies. It should be noted in this connection that Paul refers to the time of the rapture as the day of redemption (Eph. 1:14; 4:30; Rom. 8:23). Israel's day of redemption will be when Christ comes back to earth and delivers them from all their enemies. Our day of redemption will be when Christ comes in the air and catches us up to be with Him in our resurrection bodies.

We therefore believe that God alone through our Lord Jesus Christ has made a perfect and complete provision of salvation which is sufficient for all mankind from Adam down to the last man that shall be born. We further believe that in God's dispensational program redemption for Israel involves not only forgiveness of sins but also deliverance from political enemies and from diseases and other material troubles; whereas for members of the Body of Christ its blessings are purely spiritual, with promise of a future day of the redemption of the body.

The Application of Salvation
Unlimited Provision, Limited Application

In stating our beliefs on this subject, we want it made very plain at the outset that we do not believe that the Scripture teaches that salvation will be applied to all mankind universally, and even to fallen angels and the Devil. We categorically deny the teachings of Universal Reconciliationism. We believe in an unlimited provision in salvation, but in a limited application. The Scriptures relate over and over again that some are going to be lost. They also speak of the elect, which would be a meaningless term if all were to be saved.

The Roman Catholic, the Lutheran, and many Protestant denominations may virtually agree with us on the provision of salvation--that God is its

18

Author, that Christ's blood was the price paid, that it is impossible to be saved apart from Christ. But there the agreement ends. When we ask: How is that salvation applied to the sinner? By what means does God bestow His grace upon us? then the confusion begins. The ritualist quotes such verses as Acts 2:38 and insists that repentance and water baptism are necessary prerequisites to receiving the grace of God. Sacraments have been invented by the church to be a means of grace, that is, the means whereby God bestows His grace. Many hurdles are thus put in the path of the sinner which he must clear before he reaches the place where salvation can be obtained.

Varying Requirements

We believe that faith has always been God's requirement of man. *"Without faith it is impossible to please Him,"* and that goes for all dispensations. However, in the various dispensations God's Word has required different things from man. Faith is belief and obedience to God's Word. If God's Word said: *"Bring an animal sacrifice,"* faith brought the sacrifice. If it said, *"Keep the Sabbath day,"* faith kept the Sabbath day. If it commanded circumcision or the keeping of feast days and fast days, faith did those things. Under the kingdom gospel, while Christ was a minister of the Circumcision, and at Pentecost and shortly thereafter when the kingdom was offered to Israel, God's Word commanded repentance and water baptism for the remission of sins, and the believing ones in Israel repented and were baptized for the remission of sins and then received the supernatural empowerment of the Holy Spirit.

Now the question is, What is God's Word to us? Has the dispensation changed since Abel's day, or Abraham's day, or Moses' day, or Christ's day, or Peter's day? Does intelligent and God-pleasing faith today bring animal sacrifice, or keep the Sabbath, or observe new moons and feast days, or submit to carnal ordinances such as meats and drinks and divers baptisms? Few people have trouble when it comes to answering about animal sacrifices; more have difficulty when it comes to the Sabbath and other religious observances of feasts and fasts, and most professing Christians are completely at a loss when it comes to baptism. They can understand how some command of great antiquity given to Adam or to Moses could be rescinded, but surely nothing spoken by Christ or by the Twelve could ever be changed. They seem to forget that all through the Bible, whether God's Word came to Adam or to Moses or to us, it was

19

God's Word. Doubtless the Jews of Paul's day, who lived 1500 years after the giving of the law, had the same trouble in understanding how Moses' law could be superseded, as people do today, who live 2000 years after Christ, in understanding how some of His teachings could give way to new orders. But, of course, it was not twenty centuries after Christ's day that the change came, but only a few years--in fact, within the same generation.

Requirements for Today

We believe that a new dispensation began with Paul. We believe that prior to Paul all of God's revealed purposes concerned the establishment upon this earth of the Messianic kingdom in which Israel would be the ruling nation with the Twelve apostles sitting upon its twelve judgment thrones, and with Christ sitting upon the throne of David. After Israel's official rejection of the offered kingdom under the ministry of the Twelve in the book of Acts, God raised up a new apostle and gave to him the dispensation of the grace of God, which is also called the dispensation of the mystery, because this dispensation had been hitherto hidden in God and never before revealed or promised to the sons of men.

There is just no use in trying to reconcile Peter's preaching in Acts 2:38 with Paul's teaching for the Body of Christ, because they concern two different dispensations. And when it comes to the subject now before us, namely, the Application of Salvation, we see that Paul declares that God now justifies ungodly sinners when they do nothing more than believe the gospel that Christ died for their sins, was buried and was raised again the third day. Salvation is given under Paul's gospel apart from all works of righteousness (Titus 3:5), apart from the law (Rom. 3:21), apart from covenants and Israel's intervention (Eph. 2:13), and apart from water baptism (1 Cor. 1:17). This message is perfectly adapted to the needs of the godless, heathen world of which we are all a part. The Eskimo in the frozen north and the inhabitant of the waterless desert, the sick and the dying, the poor and the rich, the civilized and the uncivilized--all can be saved upon the same simple terms: faith in a crucified and resurrected Savior.

In other words we believe literally that which Paul declares: we are saved by grace through faith, apart from works (Eph. 2:8, 9). However, lest our statement of belief should be misconstrued by some, when we speak of

20

faith we do not mean a mere mental assent to a fact of past history. The fact of Christ's death and resurrection is all important, but merely admitting the historicity of that event does not save. Faith is a positive and active trust in the Lord Jesus Christ as Savior. It is produced in the heart as a result of the Holy Spirit's working through the Word of God. It is just as real a thing as it was in the days of miracles and signs and wonders. If we may say so, faith apart from all of these outward manifestations is the greatest faith of all; for it stands wholly upon the Word of God, apart from every visible sign.

This then is what we believe about redemption: *"God justifies ungodly sinners by His grace, upon the ground of the blood of Christ, through the means of faith. This complete salvation is bestowed as the free gift of God apart from man's works."*

ETERNAL SECURITY

WE BELIEVE that "**All of the saved are eternally secure in Christ (Col. 3:1-4; Phil. 1:6; Rom. 8:1; 8:29-34; Rom. 8:38, 39; John 10:27-29; Eph. 1:13-14).**" To have eternal life is to have eternal security. A life or security which may end is a temporal life or security. It is a contradiction in terms to speak of eternal life coming to an end. No one who is finally cast into the second death ever had eternal life. The word eternal doubtless refers to a quality of existence, but it is an existence which is everlasting, unending. One might as well speak of a million years lasting perhaps but a second, as to speak of eternal life ceasing one, five or fifty years after a person is saved.

Why This Truth Is Opposed

If the Bible plainly declares that God gives to those whom He saves the free gift of eternal life (Rom. 6:23), why is it then that many professing Christians do not believe this truth, and that some even call it a damnable heresy from the pit of hell? Many reasons and explanations might be given, but we believe that the basic and underlying cause for this strange situation is the failure of the great majority of Christians to recognize the distinctive and unique revelation contained in the Pauline epistles. This is not to say that eternal life and eternal security are to be found only in Paul's writings; for both the Gospel and the Epistles of John are also outstanding in this respect, but it is only as we come into the dispensation of the grace of God, as given to Paul, to explain what God in Christ did at Calvary and what He by the Holy Spirit does when the sinner believes the gospel, that we can understand how God can give eternal life to a sinner who is personally undeserving of it both before and after he is saved. The truth of eternal life is not in any sense of the word a unique part of the revelation of the mystery, but it is in the revelation of the mystery that we find the secret of the gospel given, apart from which we could never fully understand how God could bestow eternal life wholly apart from the principle of man's own works and merits.

Two Ways of Approach

Paul himself explains the two distinct and opposite principles upon which man may approach God and by which eternal life might conceivably be granted. In Romans 2:6,7 he sets forth the *"works"* way: *"Who will render to every man according to his deeds: to them who by patient continuance in well doing seek for glory and honor and immortality, eternal life."* This is the basis of the justice of God. But Paul shows in the next chapter that as a matter of fact and experience there is not one who is seeking after God or who is doing good. Therefore this fact rules out any possibility of any man obtaining eternal life upon the basis of works. If any man ever gets eternal life it must be upon an entirely different basis. It must come as a matter of free grace and as a free gift. And that is exactly what Paul declares: *"the gift of God is eternal life through Jesus Christ our Lord."* This is the only way of obtaining eternal life: the grace way--the faith way.

These two ways are referred to again by Paul in Rom. 4:4,5: *"Now to him that worketh is the reward not reckoned of grace but of debt. But to him that worketh not, but believeth on him that justifieth the ungodly, his faith is counted for righteousness."* Approaching God on the *"work"* principle, it is evident that one would have to come to the end of life and have all of his works finished before he could know the outcome, before he could know whether he merited eternal life. There could be no sense in which such a person could possess eternal life until his works were all judged. But on the other principle, on the *"grace"* way, God can bestow eternal life upon the believer immediately, and that is exactly what the Scripture affirms. We have (present tense) eternal life. And since it has been given as a free gift of God's grace, neither its reception nor its continued possession depends in any sense upon man's merit. If it depends in any degree whatsoever upon man's merit, then God could not give it until man's merit had been completely tested and approved; for we have already seen that it is eternal in character and that it would be a contradiction on God's part to give something eternal which would later prove to be temporal.

But the big question looms in our minds: How could God give eternal life as a free gift, wholly apart from what man deserves? Or in other words: How could God be just in justifying ungodly sinners? It is this question which is so beautifully answered in the Pauline revelation of the gospel. See the context of Rom. 3:26. Every holy, righteous claim that God had against the sinner was completely satisfied by the death of His Son. He is therefore perfectly righteous in bestowing eternal life upon unworthy sinners who do nothing more than meet the simple terms of His gospel of grace--believing that Christ died for their sins, was buried, and rose again the third day. Righteous people, of course, who suppose that they have some righteousness of their own, hate and despise such a doctrine, and in their zeal would consign to perdition anyone who would teach such heresy. It reminds us of Paul's word of defense before Felix: "*But this I confess unto thee, that after the way which they call heresy, so worship I the God of my fathers*" (Acts 24:14).

So-called Anti-security Passages

"All of this sounds very logical," someone will say, "but how about all of those verses in the Bible which seem to teach just the opposite?" The Scriptures do contain many solemn warnings, but to lump them all together and say that if they mean anything at all, they teach the believer's possibility of being lost, is to show very little intelligence in handling the Word of God. These warnings may be classified under the following heads:

1. *Those applying to some other dispensation.* Many of the warnings from the Old Testament and Gospels have to do not with soul salvation but with the physical consequences of breaking the law. See Ezekiel 33:13. The curse of a broken law brought physical death upon many who were no doubt saved people. Saints today die physically because of the course of sin that is in their bodies, but that does not mean that they are not saved. Other warnings, such as Matthew 18:23-35; 24:13; 25:30; etc., refer to a time after the church is taken out of the world.

2. *Those applying to unregenerate teachers of the last day* (1 Timothy 4:1,2; 2 Peter 2:1-22; Jude 17-19; etc.). Churches are filled with such preachers today. They never were saved.

3. *Those applying to rewards and not to salvation* (1 Corinthians 3:11-15; 9:24-27; 2 Corinthians 5:9,10; Colossians 3:24,25). Salvation is entirely apart from all of man's good works. It is therefore by grace. Rewards are given for faithfulness after we are saved.

4. *Those that warn believers of things they may lose.* Believers are in danger of losing many blessings which the Lord has provided for them. Any sin, disobedience, lack of faith, neglect of the Word of God, or prayerlessness is bound to result in loss of joy, loss of power, loss of fruitfulness, loss of fellowship, and loss of reward. Typical of such warnings is Colossians 2:4,8,18. God's method of meeting such failures on the part of His own people is to chasten them, see 1 Corinthians 11:32; Hebrews 12:5-11. He does not chasten the unbeliever.

24

5. *Those that warn unbelievers.* Romans 11:21 is not a warning lest God would cast away some of His own saints, but is a warning to the Gentiles, who at present have a place of great spiritual privilege, that their continued unbelief will cause them to be cast out just as God cast out the nation of Israel. The Israelites before this time were the branches of the good olive tree, but that did not mean that every Israelite was saved; for many were Christ rejecters and because of that they were broken off. The nations have been grafted in, but the nations as such are not saved. But the day is coming when the nations will be broken off and Israel will be restored to her former position. If Paul were here speaking of personal salvation we would be forced to conclude that the natural branches which were broken off were men like Judas Iscariot and that the day is coming when Judas is to be resaved and grafted back into the tree. This passage is not dealing with personal salvation, but with national privilege.

6. *Those that prove Christian profession by fruitbearing* (John 8:31; 15:6; 1 Cor. 15:1, 2; Hebrews 3:6,14; James 2:14-26; 2 Peter 1:10; Colossians 1:23). If there has been the work of regeneration in the heart there is bound to be a manifestation of that new divine life, just as surely as the newborn babe will cry or give some other indication that it is alive.

If such passages as Heb. 6:4-6; 10:26,27; Col. 1:21-23, Gal. 5:4; John 15:6 and Matt. 24:13 are studied dispensationally and grammatically in their context, it will be seen that they do not militate in any way against the truth that all true believers actually do have as a present and an eternal possession, eternal life.

33 Scriptural Proofs of Security

On the positive side, the fact of eternal security is seen to rest upon the following facts of divine revelation:

1. If we through real saving faith have believed on the Son of God we have ETERNAL LIFE, and shall never perish nor come into condemnation (John 3:16,36; 5:24; 6:40,47; 10:28; Romans 8:1; 1 John 5:12,13).
2. We have been born of God, and whatsoever is born of God overcometh the world (John 3:3; 1 Peter 1:23; 1 John 5:4,5).
3. We are God's workmanship, and whatsoever God doeth it shall be forever (Eph. 2:10; Eccl. 3:14).
4. God is able to perform to completion that good work which

25

He has begun in us (Phil. 1:6).

5. We are kept by God's power (1 Peter 1:5; Jude 24).

6. Christ as the great High-priest pledges Himself to save to the uttermost ALL who come unto God by Him, and He is able; for He lives for ever to make intercession for them (Heb. 7:25; Rom. 8:34).

7. God has promised not to allow His children to be tempted in excess of what they are able to bear, and the Lord knoweth how to deliver the godly out of temptation (1 Cor. 10:13; 1 Peter 2:9).

8. Every true child of God is indwelt by the Holy Spirit, and He is more powerful than any foe (1 John 4:4) .

9. The Father is greater than ALL, and no one has power to pluck us out of His hand (John 10:29).

10. Our Lord Jesus has already obtained ETERNAL redemption for us (Heb. 9:12).

11. He is the Author of ETERNAL salvation, and the Author and Finisher of our faith (Heb. 5:8; 12:2).

12. He gives this eternal salvation to us as a free gift which He Himself has already fully paid for. We did not deserve the gift in the first place, and therefore He will not take it from us if we remain undeserving (Rom. 6:23; 5:20; 1 Pet. 1:19).

13. Sin is what separates us from God, and God has already forgiven us ALL trespasses (Col. 2:13).

14. We are not saved by our works of righteousness, and therefore a lack of such works cannot cause the loss of salvation (Titus 3:5; Eph. 2:8; Rom. 3:28; 4:6).

15. Christ is our foundation, and that foundation standeth sure (1 Cor. 3:11; 2 Tim. 2:19).

16. He has promised: *"I will never leave thee, nor forsake thee"* (Heb.13:5) .

17. Christ said: *"ALL that the Father giveth me shall come to me; and him that cometh to me I will in no wise cast out .... And this is the Father's will which hath sent me that of ALL which he hath given me I should lose NOTHING .... No man can come to me except the Father which hath sent me draw him"* (John 6:37,39,44). The logic of this is overwhelming. If salvation is ever lost, Christ, and not we, will lose it.

18. Christ promised: *"And I will pray the Father, and he shall give you another Comforter, that he may abide with you FOREVER,* even *the Spirit of truth"* (John 14:16). Could a person be lost, and still have the Holy Spirit abiding with him forever?

19. We are called of God, and have been given the gift of eternal

26

life (Rom. 8:29,30; 6:23). "*The gifts and calling of God are without repentance*" (Rom. 11:29).

20. Christ has washed us from our sins in His own blood (Rev. 1:5), and "*He that is washed--clean every whit*" (John 13: 10) .

21. God is able to make His weakest child to stand. "*Yea, he shall be holden up; for God is able to make him stand*" (Rom. 14:4) .

22. Even if we fail and are unfaithful, "*yet He abideth faithful: He cannot deny Himself*" (2 Tim. 2:13).

23. God will not impute sins to His children (Rom. 4:8). When we sin, He will chasten us that we be not condemned with the world (1 Cor.11:32).

24. All who have believed in Christ were chosen of God before the foundation of the world, that they should be holy and without blame before Him in love (Eph.1:4). It is impossible to suppose that God's eternal purposes will ever fail.

25. Christ has already bought every member of His church, and He will surely get for His own glory all whom He has purchased (1 Cor. 6:20; Eph. 5:25-27).

26. We who believe will never come into judgment (John 5:24; Rom. 8:1), because Christ has already borne our judgment. In God's sight we have already been put to death for our sins in the person of our Substitute, and therefore all of the righteous claims of God's law against us have been eternally satisfied, and we have been freed from sin and from the law (Gal. 2:19,20; Rom. 6:2-10; 7:4). God is not unrighteous. He will not demand a double payment for sins.

27. The believer is not under the law but under grace, and therefore sin cannot have dominion over him (Rom. 6:14).

28. If God could say that He had not beheld iniquity in Jacob, neither had seen perverseness in Israel, in spite of their murmurings and sins (Num. 23:21), surely He can say as much of redeemed sinners made accepted in the Beloved (Eph. 1:6) .

29. If God be for us, as He most surely is, no one can prevail against us (Rom. 8:31).

30. No one will ever be able to condemn or bring charge against one whom God has justified (Rom. 8: 32-34) .

31. Nothing or no one will ever be able to separate us from the love of God that is in Christ Jesus our Lord (Rom. 8:39) .

32. If we sin after we are saved (and who does not?), we have an Advocate with the Father, Jesus Christ the Righteous (1 John 2:1), and He is a Lawyer who has never lost a case. This is amply illustrated in Luke

22:31,32, where Christ prayed for Peter that his faith fail not, even as He prays for all of His own (John 17: 20).

33.The work of the Holy Spirit of God guarantees eternal salvation to every believer. He is regenerated or born again by the Holy Spirit into the family of God (John 1:12, 13; 3:5; Titus 3:5). He is indwelt forever by the Holy Spirit (John 14:16; 1 Cor. 6:19). He is baptized by the Spirit into the Body of Christ (1 Cor. 12:13), thus having effected a permanent relationship in that Body. He is sealed with that Holy Spirit of promise until the redemption of the purchased possession (Eph. 1:13, 14; 4:30), which guarantees his security until that day of manifestation in glory with Christ.

Practical Effects of Security Teaching

In conclusion we must consider the practical effect of this teaching upon the life of the Christian. Those who oppose eternal security charge that it leads to carelessness, indifference, and licentiousness. This is exactly what would happen if the truth of eternal security were given to a natural, unregenerate soul. And this charge is a withering indictment against those who make it that they know nothing of the experience of the new life in Christ Jesus. The true Christian is one who has been regenerated, has the Holy Spirit indwelling his body, and is motivated by heavenly principles. While he still has the nature of the flesh within him, to which he may at times yield, and against which he is warned in such passages as Gal. 5:13, he is a new creation in Christ, and nothing could be more conducive to a godly, consecrated life than to know and to appreciate the wonderful riches of His grace in bestowing upon him eternal life through Jesus Christ our Lord. One might as well argue that it is a very dangerous thing to repeat the marriage vows; for the wife, having been endowed with all of the worldly goods of her husband, will immediately rush out and squander them upon her own selfish lusts. This has happened in cases where a woman's motive in marriage was money instead of love, but the true child of God is one who loves the Lord Jesus Christ (1 Cor.16:22), and the more he knows of the truth of security the more his love will abound. The unregenerate soul can conceive no other motive for obedience but fear of punishment. The regenerate soul cries out with Paul: *"The love of Christ constrains us...that they which live should not henceforth live unto themselves, but unto him which died for them, and rose again."*

THE HOLY SPIRIT

IN a previous chapter we clearly confessed belief in one God, eternally existing in three Persons: Father, Son and Holy Spirit. Now we wish to set forth what we believe concerning the Personality and Work of the Holy Spirit.

"The Holy Spirit is a Person Who convicts the world of sin, and Who regenerates, baptizes, seals, indwells, enlightens and empowers the saved (John 16:8; Titus 3:5; 1 Corinthians 12:13; Ephesians 1:13, 17, 18; 3:16)."

His Person

We must repeat to the point of becoming tiresome perhaps that we are unalterably opposed to the teaching of certain dispensationalists, such as the Concordant Version people, who deny the Personality of the Holy Spirit. Certain of our shallow-minded critics reason that if we share somewhat similar views on dispensationalism with the Concordants, we must of necessity follow them in denying the truth of the Trinity and the correlative truth of the Personality of the Holy Spirit. Some have even gone as far as to charge us with subterfuge in denying this false doctrine; others have charged that dispensationalism inevitably leads to Unitarianism and Universalism as held by the Concordant group, when, as a matter of fact, there is not the slightest connection between these doctrines. This is evident from the fact that the great majority of those who have taught Unitarianism or Universalism in the history of the church never had the slightest apprehension of dispensational truth. The fact is that among both Unitarians and Trinitarians have been numbered Universalists and Annihilationists, Dispensationalists and Anti-dispensationalists. One might just as well argue that because Roman Catholics believe in the Trinity everyone else who believes in the Trinity will be inevitably led into the teachings of Mariolatry, purgatory, the mass, baptismal regeneration, and popery. We believe in the personality of the Holy Spirit because the Scriptures give to Him all of the attributes of personality as well as the attributes of deity.

His Work

In considering the work of the Holy Spirit it is most important to see that there are some ministries which are unique in relation to the Body of

29

Christ and some which are common to all of the redeemed. We feel that some dispensationalists have erred in supposing that it would be either impossible or inconsistent to believe, for example, that the Holy Spirit would perform the work of the new birth upon both believing Israelites under the kingdom dispensation and also upon believing sinners in this dispensation of the grace of God. On the other hand, we believe that others, such as the Pentecostalists, err greatly in supposing that all of the works which the Holy Spirit wrought in connection with the kingdom program must of necessity be in evidence today. They claim that if the Holy Spirit appeared as cloven tongues of fire at Israel's Pentecost, so He must do today; if the Jewish apostles had to wait for the promised baptism of the Spirit, so we must do today; if the Spirit once gave miraculous gifts of tongues, miracles and healings, so He must do today. The only solution to this problem is a sane, sensible, Spirit-led right division of the Word of Truth. When this is done we believe that it will be seen that certain of the Spirit's ministries are for all of the redeemed of both the kingdom and the grace dispensations, and some are peculiar to either one or the other of these administrations.

Because of the nature of the natural man, whether he be Jew or Gentile, under this or another dispensation, we believe that the convicting, quickening work of the Holy Spirit is absolutely essential before the sinner will believe on the Lord Jesus Christ. Paul makes it very clear in Eph. 2:1-3 that all, both Jews and Gentiles, were personally dead in trespasses and sins, although Israel nationally, in times past, by reason of the covenants, was near to God, whereas the Gentiles were far off. Some have supposed that the Israelites personally had a different kind of nature from the Gentiles, that they possessed some kind of spiritual life, and that they therefore needed only a new birth, whereas the Gentiles were dead in sins and needed, not a new birth, but to be made new creatures. On the basis of such reasoning it has been taught that the new birth is for Israel and the new creation is for us today. This reasoning, however, is very faulty. If there is one thing evident from the first three chapters of Romans, it is that God's dealings with Israel under the law proved that there was no difference between the Jew and the Gentile as touching their sinful natures. Surely no one would argue that there is a difference today between the Jew and the Gentile spiritually by nature. If we are to believe that there was a difference in the past dispensation, then we must find a place in history when all of the Jewish people died spiritually and became as Gentiles. Such a notion is foreign to the Scriptures. But the Scriptures do plainly teach that Israel as a nation fell from its place of covenanted privilege when God inaugurated this great ministry of reconciliation under the dispensation of the grace of God (Rom.11:7-25).

Regeneration

If Jews and Gentiles both possessed the same kind of sinful, fallen nature, then in order to become children of God they need the same kind of work done to them by the Spirit of God. John 3:3 teaches the necessity of the new birth for an Israelite. Titus 3:5 teaches the necessity of the new birth or regeneration for Jew or Gentile today. Whereas both the Jew and the Gentile under both the kingdom and the grace dispensations stand in need of the same work of regeneration by the Spirit, it is evident that believers under these two dispensations have a different religious and spiritual program. God may have required ceremonial baptism as an act of faith in other dispensations, as an accompaniment of regeneration, but He has no such requirement today. Some of our grace brethren may feel that being "born of water and of the Spirit" in John 3:5 refers to water baptism in connection with the work of the Spirit, but it should be noticed that under Paul, who was not sent to baptize, regeneration is also connected with washing and water (Titus 3:5 cf. Eph. 5:26). Here the washing is surely not with literal water, but the water of the Word. Many of the grace brethren, while acknowledging that water baptism was being practiced for the remission of sins while Jesus was on earth, feel that the water in John 3:5 is the same as in Eph. 5:26.

Baptism

The baptizing work of the Holy Spirit needs also to be studied dispensationally. John the Baptist announced that Christ would baptize with the Holy Spirit (Matt. 3:11), and this doubtless took place on the day of Pentecost (Acts 1:5). This baptizing was done by Christ and resulted in the empowering of the apostles to do miraculous works. Since Peter declared that this miraculous outpouring of the Holy Spirit was that which Joel had prophesied about 800 years previously, it should be evident that this Spirit baptism could not be identical with the work described in 1 Cor. 12:13; for if anything is plainly stated in Paul's epistles, it is that the truth about the Body of Christ was a secret which was never before made known to the sons of men in other ages and generations. It would be strange indeed if the prophets should have so much to say about the very

31

work of the Spirit which forms the Body of Christ and at the same time be ignorant of the fact that there was even to be a Body of Christ.

In the Spirit baptism which forms the Body of Christ, it is not Christ baptizing with the Spirit, as happened at Pentecost, but the Holy Spirit baptizing into Christ. We must not confuse the Persons of the Trinity, and yet that is exactly what they do who make these two Spirit baptisms one and the same; for they have Christ baptizing into Christ.

Another difference between these two baptizing works is seen in the fact that the one which is a part of the Pauline revelation results in the joining together of Jews and Gentiles as joint-members of a joint-body; whereas at Pentecost the message was to Jews only and it continued that way for several years. Surely there was not a joint-body at Pentecost. Had Gentiles been brought into joint relationship with the Jews at Pentecost, Peter's "sheet-vision" would have been unnecessary. How could Peter's words to Cornelius be explained: "*It is an unlawful thing for a man that is a Jew to keep company, or come unto one of another nation,*" if God some eight years before had dissolved the difference between Jew and Gentile and had made them joint-sharers? And how could the objections raised by the Jerusalem saints to Peter's preaching to a Gentile be explained (Acts 11: 2,3), if in fact at Pentecost, and all the years that followed after, the gospel had been preached to the Gentiles?

There is no place here to plead the argument that perhaps God secretly began the Body at Pentecost but did not make known the fact until He revealed it to Paul many years later. The fact is that there just was no joint-body until some Gentiles as such were saved, and we know that could not have been until the salvation of Cornelius at least. Nor can we accept the commonly held *Baptist view* that Spirit baptism took place only twice, once at Pentecost where Jews corporately were put in the Body and once in Cornelius' house, where Gentiles corporately were placed in the Body. Thus they argue that Spirit baptism has ceased, and the one baptism left for the Body (Eph. 4:5) is water baptism. It is most difficult to understand how one with the slightest insight into the doctrinal progress of the New Testament could suppose that in this dispensation of the grace of God the work of the Spirit ceases, leaving us only with a ceremonial ritual. If anything is evident from the pages of the epistles it is that the ritual has given place to the spiritual. And that is exactly what we of the Grace Movement believe: that the ritual baptism has ceased, leaving us with the one baptism which is spiritual; not the Spirit's baptism in miraculous powers as at Pentecost, but the Spirit's baptism of believing Jews and Gentiles into the Body of Christ.

Sealing and Indwelling

The work of the Spirit in sealing, indwelling, enlightening and empowering the saved is not necessarily dispensational in nature. That is, we find the Spirit doing these ministries for both those under the kingdom dispensation and for those under the present dispensation. The sealing by the Spirit, whether it be the 144,000 Israelites in Rev. 7:4, or the members of the Body of Christ in Eph. 1:13, is a guarantee of safe-keeping and of final deliverance. This ministry of the Spirit is one of the basic factors in the glorious truth of the eternal security of the saved.

The Spirit's indwelling in all believers is dispensational in that it was not true before the day of Pentecost, but since that time it is doubtless true of all believers in Christ. Christ made the promise of the Spirit's indwelling in the believer in John 14:16,17 to Israel's apostles, and of course it is abundantly clear from Paul's epistles for today that if any man have not the Spirit of Christ, he is none of His (Rom. 8:9). We therefore believe that the third Person of the divine Trinity, the Holy Spirit, after convicting the sinner, regenerates him upon believing, and at the same instant baptizes him into the Body of Christ, seals him unto the day of redemption, and indwells his body permanently as long as this life shall last. We believe that apart from the enlightening and empowering work of the indwelling Spirit, it is impossible for the believer to understand the Word of God or to live a life pleasing to God. We believe that it is our Christian duty to be filled with the Spirit and to manifest the fruit of the Spirit, but since this subject is covered in a separate statement in our doctrinal platform, we will await a future chapter to discuss further what we believe about the Christian's walk.

33

THE CHURCH

"IN THE present dispensation there is only one true Church, which is called the Body of Christ (1 Cor. 12:13; Eph. 1:22,23; 3:6). The historical manifestation of the Body of Christ began with the Apostle Paul before he wrote his first epistle (1 Thess. 2:14-16 cf. Acts 13:45, 46; Phil. 1:5, 6 cf. Acts 16; 1 Cor. 12:13,27 cf. Acts 18)."

This is briefly what we believe about the church. There is much more, however, which needs to be said in order to bring out many of the distinctive truths connected with this subject.

Meaning of the Word

Our English word *church* is a very general term. It means nothing specific. To some it means a building used for religious purposes; to others it is just the so-called sanctuary of such a building; to others it signifies a religious denomination; while to yet others it has the more scriptural significance of a company of God's people. The English word *church* is no doubt a very poor translation of the original Bible word, *ekklesia*, which means a called-out assembly. The word *church* is derived from the Greek word *kyriakon*, which is the possessive form of the word *Lord*. It therefore means the Lord's or belonging to the Lord. It should be evident therefore that to use a word meaning *the Lord's* to translate a word meaning *a called-out assembly* is very poor translation. In fact, the translators themselves were forced to give *ekklesia* its true meaning in Acts 19:32,39 for there the word describes an ungodly multitude which assembled to persecute Paul and his companions.

More Than One Church

To understand the Bible doctrine of the church, then, it is first of all necessary to know that the Bible word has no reference to a building or to a denomination, but to an assembly of people called out for some specific purpose. But something further is necessary. It must be recognized that not every occurrence of the word in the Bible refers to the same called-out company. Of course, this fact is evident from the passage just referred to in Acts 19. But the great majority of Fundamentalists seem to have the impression that when the word is used religiously there is only one church in the Bible. And then there is the further mistaken idea that there was no church in Old Testament times. Acts 7:38 should be sufficient evidence to prove that there was a church in Moses' day, for Israel is there called *the church in the wilderness*. Of course, the Old Testament was written in Hebrew and so we could hardly expect to find the Greek word *ekklesia* in it. However, the translators of the Septuagint chose to use the word *ekklesia* some seventy times to translate the Hebrew word *kahal*, or congregation. The majority of the Jews of New Testament times used the Septuagint version, and therefore they would read about the *ekklesia* or church of God many times in their old Scriptures.

In the light of the above facts it must be admitted that Israel was called an *ekklesia* or church in Old Testament times. But this is still not sufficient. Many will contend that while the above facts are true, wherever we read the word *ekklesia* in the New Testament it always refers to the New Testament church of this present dispensation. Therefore the church in Matt.16:18; 18:17; Acts 2:47; Revelation 1:20 is the identical church or Body of Christ of which Paul speaks many times in his epistles. As long as one persists in this error and fails to see the distinction between the church which is His Body (Eph.1:22,23), and the prophesied church of the kingdom in Matthew and Revelation, he is bound to bring great confusion into church doctrine for today.

Had the church fathers rightly divided the Word of truth in Matt. 16:18,19, Rome would never have had a leg to stand upon. Protestants as a general rule go right along with Rome and agree that the church in this passage is the church of this dispensation, and then they try to refute Rome's claim to the powers of binding and loosing. It should be noticed that the same powers of binding and loosing are mentioned in connection with the church in Matt. 18:18,19. If we but simply recognize the fact that this church is connected with the kingdom of the heavens, as Christ Himself plainly states in Matt. 16:19, and if we have understood the very elemental truth that the kingdom of the heavens is the yet future Messianic kingdom to be set up on the earth under Messiah's rule, we will see that no religious organization today has the right to apply these passages to itself. These powers of binding and loosing are going to be exercised in the future kingdom when the Twelve apostles sit upon twelve thrones judging the twelve tribes of Israel (Matt. 19:28).

The Body of Christ Church

But it may be asked, "What evidence is there to prove that the church in Paul's epistles is a different company from that in Matthew or in the early part of the Acts?" If this fact can be established from the Scripture, then it at once proves erroneous the old idea that the same church has continued in existence from Adam, and the more generally held view in Fundamentalism that the church of Matthew and Pentecost is the Body of Christ church.

We have already given one evidence, namely that the church of Matthew is a part of the Messianic kingdom of the heavens which will be set up on earth after the church of this dispensation has had its last member added to it and it has been raptured to glory. Everyone who is a Premillennialist and who believes that the church is some day to be completed and raptured, must believe that this will take place before the second coming of Christ to earth to establish His kingdom, wherein the Twelve will have their judgment thrones and exercise their power as judges. There is surely no question about all of the people who comprise both of the churches being saved, redeemed saints; but the fact that one of the groups is to be completed and in heaven while the other is on earth and still functioning in the matter of growth is sufficient evidence to prove that there is a difference between them.

Perhaps the most evident distinction, however, is the fact that the church of Matthew and of Pentecost is one which was prophesied or predicted by the Old Testament prophets, whereas the church of Paul's epistles is specifically declared to be a part of a great body of truth which in former ages had been hidden in God and never before revealed to the sons of men (Eph. 3:5,9; Col.1:24-26). Ps. 22:22, as quoted in Heb. 2:12, is evidence that there was a church predicted in the Old Testament scripture. The kingdom of the heavens with which this church is connected is one of the main burdens of prophecy. The words of the Spirit-filled apostle in Acts 3:21,24 show that everything that was happening at Pentecost and thereafter was in fulfillment of the prophets. Now if that which was spoken by the mouth of all of the prophets is identically the same as that which was hidden in God and never made known to the prophets, we can logically say that the two churches under consideration are the same. If the above language indicates a difference, then we must say that there is a difference.

36

One has but to compare the main characteristics of the church which is Christ's Body with those of the kingdom church to see the difference. Paul sums up the truth about the Body of Christ in Eph. 3:6 by showing that it is a body in which Jews and Gentiles are joint-heirs, in a joint-body, and are joint-partakers of His promise in Christ by the gospel whereof Paul (in contrast to the Twelve) had been made a minister. Now if we examine the church which existed in Acts 2 and 3 we will discover that it is entirely Israelitish; that there is no hint of a joint relationship of Jews and Gentiles in it either as to doctrine or to actual fact and that Paul, to whom the revelation of the Body and of the present dispensation was made, was not even saved as yet.

Body Church a Mystery

The Old Testament plainly predicted salvation for the Gentiles, but as Dr. Scofield so aptly points out in his footnote on page 1252 of his Reference Bible, *"That the Gentiles were to be saved was no mystery* (Rom. 9: 24-33; 10:19-21).*The mystery 'hid in God' was the divine purpose to make of Jew and Gentile a wholly new thing--'the church, which is his (Christ's) body,' formed by the baptism with the Holy Spirit* (1 Cor. 12:12,13) *and in which the earthly distinctions of Jew and Gentile disappear* (Eph. 2:14,15; Col. 3:10,11)."* And then Dr. Scofield falls back into the old basic error of exegesis and tells us that the revelation of this mystery which was committed to Paul was foretold by Christ in Matt. 16:18. But then he goes on to state a further truth: *"in his [Paul's] writings alone we find the doctrine, position, walk, and destiny of the church."*

Body Church Addressed in All Paul's Letters

Thus far we have given Scriptural evidence for our belief that the church which is Christ's Body, the church of this dispensation, is a separate and distinct company of God's redeemed ones, having of course a basic unity in Christ as the Savior of all mankind who become saved in any dispensation, but having a calling, position and walk different from the saints of other dispensations and having part in a distinct and separate body from them. It is now necessary for us to show that there is only one church in view in all of Paul's epistles; for there are some dispensationalists who contend that Paul, all during the history of the book of Acts, was a minister of the same kingdom church that we saw in existence on the day of Pentecost, and that then, after Acts 28:28, God began the church which is Christ's Body. According to this view the church in Romans, 1 and 2 Corinthians, Galatians, and 1 and 2 Thessalonians was a kingdom church, and only in Ephesians, Philippians and Colossians do we find a reference to the church of this present dispensation. We wish to make it very plain that we do not in any sense of the word embrace any such teaching--in fact, we believe it is a dangerous error and we do all we can to combat it. We believe that the Body of Christ had its historical beginning with the ministry of Paul before he wrote his first epistle. We recognize that there was a transition going on in the latter half of the book of Acts, from the kingdom to the Body dispensation, and we believe that there is a significance to Paul's action   in pronouncing blindness upon Israel in Acts 28. We believe that the end of Acts marks the end of the transition period, and the passing away, as far as God's designed program for the Body is concerned, of everything Israelitish including the sign gifts and water baptism.

The Body and the Transition

If there was such a thing as a transition period, and we believe that there was, then the present dispensation must have begun with the beginning of the transition and have gradually emerged from the old, and must have been in full manifestation at the end of the transition. Analogies from nature and from the Scriptures show that God always brings such changes through transition. There is a transition from night to day and from day to night every twenty-four hours. The day actually begins with the first shafts of morning light and the transition period of dawn ends with the full rising of the sun and the blotting out of the stars and of the last vestige of darkness upon the horizon. Paul's earlier and later epistles are full of internal evidences of an organic unity which testify to the truth of the fact that the people saved under Paul's ministry during the Acts were still in the same Body of Christ after the Acts period. For example, consider the Philippians, saved in Acts 16, to whom Paul writes after Acts in Phil. 1:5,6, *"For your fellowship in the gospel from the first day until now; Being confident of this very thing, that he which hath begun a good work in you will perform it until the day of Jesus Christ."* If any change in their calling or hope or position had taken place since the day they were saved in Acts 16, Paul didn't know anything about it. In many other places in this book will be found further answers to this error which splits Paul's ministry and his epistles into two distinct dispensations.

38

Having shown from Scripture that the church of this present dispensation is separate and distinct from the churches of other dispensations (God has always had His church or called-out ones), and that it had its historical beginnings, not with Peter on Pentecost but with Paul's ministry, and that the church to which Paul ministered during Acts was the same to which he ministered until his death and the same which still exists today, it remains only to say that we believe that all true believers since Paul's day to the present time, regardless of membership or lack of membership in a local church organization, regardless of having had or not having had the ceremony of baptism practiced upon them, and regardless of whether or not they knew or comprehended the fact, have been baptized by one Spirit into the one Body of Christ. God alone knows who the saved ones are, but we believe that they are all in God's sight members of the same body, and that the crying need is to get back to the great Pauline doctrine of the One Body and to endeavor to keep the unity of the Spirit in the bond of peace.

MINISTRY GIFTS

THE ministry gifts for the Body of Christ are enumerated in Ephesians 4:7-11; Romans 12:6-8; 1 Corinthians 12:1-31. Some of these gifts were permanent in nature and some were to pass away; some were of the nature of ministers given to the Church and some were individual enablements for spiritual services. Since the New Testament canon was completed through the ministries of Apostles and Prophets, we believe these two offices have been fulfilled and no longer exist. Likewise the sign gifts, such as tongues, miracles, and healing, which were addressed primarily to the nation of Israel (1 Cor. 14:22) have fulfilled their purpose and have passed away according to 1 Corinthians 13:8-11.

Eph. 4:7-16 reads as follows: *"But unto every one of us is given grace according to the measure of the gift of Christ. Wherefore he saith, When he ascended up on high, he led captivity captive, and gave gifts unto men. (Now that he ascended, what is it but that he also descended first into the lower parts of the earth? He that descended is the same also that ascended up far above all heavens, that he might fill all things.) And he gave some, apostles; and some, prophets, and some, evangelists; and some, pastors and teachers, for the perfecting of the saints, for the work of the ministry, for the edifying of the body of Christ: till we all come in the unity of the faith, and of the knowledge of the Son of God, unto a perfect man, unto the measure of the stature of the fulness of Christ: that we henceforth be no more children, tossed to and fro, and carried about with every wind of doctrine, by the sleight of men, and cunning craftiness, whereby they lie in wait to deceive; but speaking the truth in love may grow up into him in all things, which is the head, even Christ: from whom the whole body fitly joined together and compacted by that which every joint supplieth, according to the effectual working in the measure of every part, maketh increase of the body unto the edifying of itself in love."*

Sign Gifts or Ministry Gifts?

These ministry gifts which are given for the edification of the Body of Christ stand in contrast with the miraculous sign gifts which were in evidence during the period covered by the book of Acts and which are mentioned in 1 Cor.12:28-30. After the apostles, prophets and teachers come miracles, healings, helps, governments, tongues and interpretation of tongues. The question naturally arises, should we have these gifts of miracle working, healing, tongues and interpretation of tongues in the church today? It would appear that more and more are swinging over to the notion that we should have them, and various movements are under way to try to discover why we do not have them and to seek means to restore them to the church. The modern Pentecostal movement, of course, spearheads this effort, although many on the sidelines are lending encouragement to the idea. Some magazines, such as *Christian Life*, have printed numerous editorials and articles questioning why the church does not possess these gifts today and suggesting that Christians pray and tarry and strive to get these gifts back. We believe that the Scripture contains the answer to this problem and that we do not have to resort to doubts and speculations or to the outbursts of emotionalism for our guidance. We believe that the Scripture plainly indicates the purpose of these sign-gifts, that it teaches that when the purpose of these gifts was realized the gifts would cease, and we believe that the purpose was realized long ago, at the end of the Acts period, and that there was a cessation of the gifts at that time.

Since Paul singles out the gift of tongues to illustrate his teachings in 1 Cor. 14, we will follow the same method. First, he shows that tongues are for a *"sign"* (vs. 22). He has told us earlier that *"the Jews require a sign."* God has always dealt in signs with the Jewish nation from the day when He called them out of Egypt. Jesus did many signs when He was in their midst (John 20:30). On this point Paul hopes that we will not be children in understanding, but that we will be mature (vs. 20). In vs. 21 he says: *"In the law (of Moses) it is written, With men of other tongues and other lips will I speak to this people (Israel)...Wherefore tongues are for a sign."* It should be evident from all of this that the purpose of tongues was to give a sign to unbelieving Israel.

Sign Gifts Temporary

Paul has already told us that tongues and the other like gifts were temporary in nature and were to pass away when that which is perfect or mature has come, (1 Cor.13:8-10). The word *perfect* in 13:10 is translated *men* in 14:20 and of *full age* in Heb. 5:14. It was given unto Paul to usher in the new dispensation of the grace of God. This new dispensation came in gradually while the dispensation which concerned the Messianic kingdom gradually passed away. We call this time of waxing and waning the transition period. 1 Corinthians was written during the transition period. These sign gifts which were originally a part of the spiritual program of the kingdom gospel were carried over into this transition period. As long as God was bearing a special witness to the nation of Israel this transition period continued and the sign gifts continued. When God wound up His dealings for the present with Israel, as He did in Acts 28, there was no longer any object or ministry for these signs to accomplish. We believe that at that time God withdrew these gifts. (It is not necessary to suppose that they were withdrawn all at a certain hour or on a certain day, but rather that they gradually diminished and passed away during that immediate era.) After the complete setting aside of Israel and the cessation of the sign-gifts God brought to maturity or perfection the revelation of truth for this present dispensation and we find that filling up of truth in Paul's prison epistles. Therefore when Paul enumerates the gifts in the prison epistle of Ephesians, he makes no reference to the sign gifts. We believe that this is the plain, Scriptural explanation of what happened to the sign gifts, and we further believe that when one seeks to revive them for the church today he manifests his ignorance of the purpose and will of God for this dispensation of the grace of God.

It is to be understood that the offices of apostle and of prophet were also to cease, but for a somewhat different reason. All that the apostles or the prophets had to give to the Body of Christ is now written down in the Scripture. At the time Ephesians was written there was still a ministry for the apostles and prophets to perform. That the gift of healing had ceased is evident from the fact that Paul, who before had performed every type of healing miracle, now leaves behind sick one of his most faithful workers (2 Tim. 4:20), and for another he prescribes a remedy for his oft sicknesses. Surely if Paul had the gift of healing at that time he would have exercised it upon these most faithful fellow-workers.

Modern Attempts to Revive Sign Gifts

Modern Pentecostal people put the emphasis upon tongues and even claim that one does not have the Holy Spirit if he has not spoken in tongues. Paul classifies tongues as the least of the gifts, even when it was in God's will, and says that he would rather speak five words in a known tongue than 10,000 words in an unknown one. Modern tongues people tell us that the lack of spirituality is the reason why Christians do not have these miraculous gifts today. Paul tells us that the most carnal church of his day,

42

namely that at Corinth, abounded in the gifts, and further that these gifts were bestowed in a sovereign manner by the Spirit of God. Modern tongues movements are headed up largely by women preachers, many of whom have expressed their contempt for Paul. Paul, in the very chapter where he deals with tongues, says: *"Let your women keep silence in the churches; for it is not permitted unto them to speak."* Modern tongues meetings are always a bedlam of jabbering and confusion, whereas Paul commands that only one person speak at a time; for God is not the author of confusion. Modern tongues people often have speaking in tongues without any attempt to interpret the tongues. Paul forbade anyone to speak in a tongue if there was no one present to interpret it. These and many other facts show that modern tongues movements are not operating according to the Scripture and that they are merely counterfeits of what God once bestowed upon certain believers as a sign to His ancient people of Israel.

We recognize that there are a few sincere Christians who are not Pentecostalists who agree in general that what we have said is true but who reason that perhaps under certain conditions today God may exercise His sovereign power and give to one here or there one or more of these gifts. Perhaps such gifts would be given to a missionary opening a new field of work. Such people might seek to exercise the gift of tongues in the privacy of their own room, feeling that it might come as an indication that God was putting His approval upon their spirituality. Such people might shy away from all of the emotionalism and confusion of the more rabid type of Pentecostalism, but the same answer must apply to them as it does to the most radical. We grant that God is sovereign and can do anything He wants to do and no one can stop Him. But we question whether God would go against His revealed will and Word. We know that Jesus Christ has the power to come back to earth and appear here in His glorified body at any time on any day, but although He has the sovereign power to do it, we do not believe He will exercise that sovereignty; for He has revealed that He will not come back to this earth again until the end of the great tribulation. We believe likewise that God has revealed that tongues and similar gifts have been done away for this present dispensation, and therefore we do not expect Him to exercise His sovereignty and contradict His Word in so doing.

43

Healing Under Grace

We believe in the kind of healing for today that Paul mentions in his prison epistles, but not in the gift of healing. In other words, we believe that God in His sovereign mercy heals His people in answer to prayer when it is His will, but we do not believe in divine healers. Any one who claims to have the gift of healing should read Matt.10:8: "Heal the sick, cleanse the lepers, raise the dead, cast out devils: freely ye have received, freely *give.*" This command of our Lord makes several points very plain. When the gift of healing was given it enabled the healers to raise the dead just as easily as to heal the dying. The healers were to bestow their blessing upon all of the sick freely, without price. If nothing more was said than this, modern healers would be proved unscriptural. But there is more. The power of the apostles to heal depended not upon the faith of the sick, but upon the gift of healing. When Peter and John healed the lame man at the Beautiful Gate, they did not ask him for a big offering and tell him if he had faith enough he could be healed. Instead, he was asking money from them, and they bestowed the divinely given gift freely upon him and he was immediately made whole. It would be ridiculous to say that a dead person had to exercise enough faith to be raised up, and yet the divine healers try to cover up and excuse their many failures by saying that the unhealed sick just did not have enough faith to be healed. What a travesty upon the Word of God and the work of the blessed Holy Spirit

There are many, and perhaps they are the majority, who believe that if a person can perform seemingly miraculous healings it is a proof in itself that he is truly sent of God. The great shrines of the Roman Catholic church boast as many as or more authenticated cases of healing as do the Pentecostalists. Practically every convert to Christian Science can testify to healing through Mary Baker Eddy's scheme which denies every fundamental of the Christian faith. So-called Spiritualists claim the powers of divine healing. Now if physical healing of the body is a proof of a divine work, then Roman Catholicism and Christian Science are proved to be preeminently divine, and by the same token Protestant Christianity is proved to be spiritually poverty-stricken.

We believe that the great ministry gift that is needed in the church today is that of teacher. God has given us the completed Word. That Word contains His distinctive message of grace for this present dispensation. We need teachers who can accurately and rightly divide the Word of

44

truth, so that God's people will clearly understand what in the Word is for obedience of God's people and what is not. We need teachers who not only have a technical knowledge of the Word, but who also have the Spirit of grace resting upon them. We need teachers who can teach by word and by life also what the dispensation of grace really is. Such teachers would indeed be for the perfecting or adjusting of the saints unto the work of ministering, which would result in the edifying of the Body of Christ. Our prayer is that God will give us many such men, for the conservative element in the professing church today stands in grave danger of falling headlong into the onrush of emotionalism which is sweeping along those who have not been established in the Pauline revelation of the grace of God.

THE BELIEVER'S WALK

This chapter concerns the character of the believer's walk. This is a very important subject, especially since many of our antagonists contend that too much grace leads to a life of indulgence, and that dispensationalism is a mere mental exercise that produces intellectualism instead of spirituality. We do emphasize the gospel of the grace of God and the dispensation of the mystery, but we also emphasize the fact that this truth brings with it the responsibility of the believer to live on the very highest spiritual plane. Our doctrinal statement sums up this belief in these words:

"By reason of Christ victory over sin and of His indwelling Spirit, all of the saved may and should experience deliverance from the power of sin by obedience to Rom. 6:11, but we deny that man's nature of sin is ever eradicated during this life (Rom. 6:6-14; Gal. 5:16-25; Rom. 8:37; 2 Cor. 2:14;10:2-5)."

Grace Defined

Before we can understand one another we must define our terms. Apparently many people think of grace as simply a means of getting off easily, of sliding through on the generosity of another, of absolving self of all responsibility while expecting another to assume it. To such, of course, grace is a dangerous principle. They would say that a man who takes too much grace is taking too much license; grace must lead to indulgence; liberties must be curbed; man must be placed under a strict law if any obedience is to be expected.

How different from all of this is grace in its Scriptural sense. It is so different that Rom. 6:14 declares: *"For sin shall not have dominion over you: for ye are not under the law, but under grace. What then? shall we sin, because we are not under the law, but under grace? God forbid."* This passage says at least the following things: the believer is not under the law; he is under grace; not only does grace not give any liberty to sin, but being under grace is the only condition under which the believer can be delivered from the dominion of sin; and finally to be under the law means also to be under the dominion of sin.

Grace begins at Calvary, where Jesus died for sin. Grace does not overlook sin; it judges sin and righteously pays the price of sin and puts

46

sin out of the way. The believer's life under grace is founded upon the fact that he died unto sin in the Person of a Substitute, the Lord Jesus Christ, and that he was raised up with Christ to walk in newness of life. God would never call upon a natural man to live under grace, for he would do nothing but frustrate that grace and use that grace as a means of indulging the flesh. But the believer's old man has been crucified with Christ and he thus reckons himself to be dead indeed unto sin, but alive unto God. In other words the life of grace is a life upon resurrection ground. Believers will always misuse grace when they fail to reckon themselves dead to sin. Merely writing these facts down in a doctrinal statement does not assure the believer of victory through grace--there must be the personal reckoning of our identification with Christ to be true--but grace is the only means of victory. It should be evident from all of this that even the thought of sin being granted any permission in our lives is completely foreign to the teachings of grace.

Grace-walk Is Superhuman

We believe that under grace we are expected to live, superhuman kind of life, far higher than was ever demanded by the law. But we do not believe that every Christian lives that kind of life, merely by subscribing to our doctrinal statement or that of any other group. We believe that there must be constant study of and meditation on the Word of God and constant, conscious dependence upon the power of the indwelling Holy Spirit in order to realize the victory that grace can give. We are fully aware of the dangers that beset the believer because of his old nature of sin (which is dead only by the reckoning of faith). We know that it is possible to become heady and high-minded, and to be puffed up in knowledge, but this is no peculiar trait of dispensationalists. Many who never heard of that word have become cold intellectuals in their handling of the Word of God. We know also that it is possible to turn the grace of God into lasciviousness, but that is no reason for minimizing the grace of God. We all know the dangers of counterfeiting the currency of our country, but we do not therefore. destroy our money. We rather caution one another to be observant lest we be deceived by the counterfeit. And so we believe that it is our duty constantly to teach and preach the grace of God, to so indoctrinate believers with the true meaning and the full responsibility of a life under grace that they will be enabled to discern that which is contrary and to live a positive life of godliness.

47

So far from grace leading to carelessness and sinfulness, Titus 2:12 states that grace disciplines us that, denying ungodliness and worldly lusts, we should live soberly, righteously, and godly in this present age. This discipline continues throughout life. Never does the time come this side of heaven that we do not need it. God has made it possible for us not to sin, but He has not made it impossible for us to sin. As long as we are in this body the Spirit will lust against the flesh and the flesh against the Spirit. But if we walk by means of the Spirit we will not fulfill the lusts of the flesh.

Grace-walk Is Spiritual

Our walk is to be a spiritual one, which is just another way of saying that it is to be controlled by the Spirit. Many suppose that spirituality consists in being sweet and kind, in praying much, and in engaging in certain pious acts. As a matter of fact, a person may do all of these things and not be spiritual at all. Spirituality consists in being filled with the Holy Spirit, so that He produces the life of Christ within us. To be sure, true spirituality will produce the fruit of the Spirit in the life, but we believe that it is impossible to have true spirituality apart from the knowledge of the Word of truth, rightly divided. God's Spirit always works through His revealed Word, and if we are to walk circumspectly, as wise men (Eph. 5:15), it will be necessary for us to know the will of God, as revealed in His Word. Merely knowing the Bible as such is not enough; we must know it rightly divided. That is, we must know what God's particular will and instructions are for the Body of Christ in this present dispensation. We believe that particular will of God and instruction for our walk is to be found in the Pauline epistles, even as we have quoted Dr. C. I. Scofield before on Ephesians 3:6, "In his [Paul's] writings alone we find the doctrine, position, walk and destiny of the church" (Scofield Reference Bible, p. 1252). The worthy, well-balanced walk of the believer in this present dispensation is therefore dependent upon a knowledge of the revelation which Christ gave from the glory to Paul. In his epistles we are carried to the highest spiritual heights in the Bible.

Grace-walk Is Scriptural

Here are some of Paul's references to our walk: "*we also should walk in newness of life*" *(Rom.6:4);"who walk not after the flesh, but after the Spirit*" (Rom. 8:4); *"Let us walk honestly, as in the day"* (Rom.13:13);

48

"Walk in the Spirit and ye shall not fulfill the lusts of the flesh" (Gal. 5:16); *"that ye walk worthy of the vocation wherewith ye are called* (Eph. 4:1); *"walk not as other Gentiles walk* (Eph. 4:17); "And walk in love, as Christ also hath loved us" (Eph.5:2); *"walk as children of light"* (Eph. 5:8);*"See then that ye walk circumspectly"* (Eph. 5:15); *"That ye might walk worthy of the Lord unto all pleasing"* (Col. 1:10); and it is interesting here to note that this is said to be the result of being filled with the knowledge of His will in all wisdom and spiritual understanding; *"As ye have therefore received Christ Jesus the Lord, so walk ye in him"* (Col. 2:6); *"Walk in wisdom toward them that are without"* (Col.4:5); *"as ye have received of us how ye ought to walk and to please God, so ye would abound more and more"* (1 Thess.4:1); *"not walking in craftiness, nor handling the word of God deceitfully* (2 Cor. 4:2). When we consider that almost half of the occurrences of the word *walk* in the New Testament are found in Paul's epistles, and that practically all references to the actual character of the believer's walk are Pauline, we should be convinced of the necessity of being Pauline if our walk is to be worthy of the Lord. We are saved wholly by grace; our walk is entirely in the sphere of grace, and our service is the manifestation of that same grace of our Lord Jesus Christ (2 Cor. 8:7-9).

THE LORD'S SUPPER

Paul's Commission Contains the Supper

OUR belief about the Lord's Supper has been both misunderstood and misrepresented by many of our brethren in Christ. Some, because they have not been able Scripturally to answer our dispensational teachings, have resorted to misrepresentation in order to save face and to frighten others from even giving consideration to our views. Others, permeated with the fallacious idea that water baptism and the Lord's Supper are the two inseparable ordinances of the church, cannot believe that water baptism can be eliminated from the spiritual program of the church (as we do), without also eliminating the Lord's Supper. For the first group we can only hope and pray that God will convict them that it is wrong for Christians to lie about their brethren in Christ. For the others we would ask them to search the Scriptures to see whether these two things are ever mentioned together or even associated together by the Lord, or whether He ever called them the two ordinances of the church. We are sure that they will discover, instead of similarities, many contrasts--a very significant one being that Paul's commission included the Lord's Supper, but did not contain water baptism.

And then there are our ultra-dispensational brethren who do eliminate both water baptism and the Lord's Supper from the program of the church, and they criticize us for not going all the way in our dispensationalism, and some even insinuate that we hold back and hang onto a little religion in order to please men. We believe that we have a satisfactory and Scriptural answer to all of these charges, and we are sure that we can show that these brethren have gone far beyond what the Scripture teaches and have become illogical and even ridiculous in their efforts to become so unique that they must find a brand new interpretation for everything in the Bible.

The doctrinal statement of the Grace Gospel Fellowship states:

"The communion of the Lord's Supper as revealed through the Apostle Paul in 1 Corinthians 11:23-26 is for members of the Body of Christ to observe 'until He comes.'"

"There is no place in Scripture where the Lord's Supper and

50

water baptism are linked together either as ordinances or as sacraments for the Church."

Ultra-dispensationalists Eliminate the Supper

It is not that we emphasize the Lord's Supper as being essential to salvation, or necessary for Christian fellowship even, but we believe that the basis upon which the Lord's Supper has been eliminated involves serious doctrinal consequences, and of course we do not want our names associated with anything which we believe to be unscriptural. In order to illustrate the point, we want to quote from one whom we would designate as extreme in his dispensational views. He gives three reasons why Christians in this dispensation should not observe the Lord's Supper.*

Not Lawful

First, he says, *"It is not lawful,"* and then he quotes Ex.12:43,45,48 to the effect that no uncircumcised person was to eat of the Passover and therefore no Gentile has the right to partake of the Lord's Supper. It is simply subterfuge and misrepresentation to say that the Lord's Supper is the Passover. The Passover was celebrated for fifteen centuries before there was a Lord's Supper. Neither is there any Scriptural evidence that the Lord's Supper took the place of the Passover. But that is not all. If the contention of this brother is true, then Paul is proved to be a transgressor. If anything is simple and self-evident it is that the church at Corinth was composed of both Jews and Gentiles who had been baptized by one Spirit into one body. Immediately after instructing these people how they should observe the Lord's Supper in Ch. 11, Paul says in Ch. 12:2, *"Ye know that ye were Gentiles."* Now if it was unlawful for a Gentile to eat the Lord's Supper, it is evident that Paul was instructing these Gentiles to do an unlawful thing. Let us be honest with God's people. Who is wrong on this point: the Apostle Paul, or the ones who claim that Gentiles have no right to eat the Lord's Supper? Do we have any right to call ourselves Pauline if we make out Paul to be a transgressor and instead follow some twentieth century teacher?

---

* *Truth for Today,* Sept., 1954.

51

A New Covenant Ceremony

The second reason given for not observing the Supper is: *"It has to do with the New Covenant,"* and we are informed that since that covenant was made with the house of Israel and the house of Judah, Gentiles can have no part in it. Of course, we know that both the Old and the New Covenants were made with Israel, but do not these brethren know that Paul teaches in Rom. 3:19-21 that although the Old Covenant was made only with Israel, God gave it in order to prove the whole Gentile world guilty before God? God selected one nation upon which to perform His experiment of the law, in order to prove that all nations were guilty, in much the same way that a doctor takes a sample of blood from the patient to test the entire blood stream. We have already shown that Paul ministered that which represented the blood of the New Covenant to Gentiles at Corinth who were members of the Body of Christ. In 2 Corinthians Paul calls himself an able minister of the New Covenant and proceeds to unfold the glorious truths of reconciliation (which in the Roman letter he shows to be a result of Israel's fall), and of the New Creation, which are surely part and parcel of God's spiritual truth for this dispensation. The blessings of the New Covenant are spiritual in nature, and Paul tells the Gentiles in Rom. 15:27 that they have been made partakers of Israel's spiritual things. What spiritual things did Israel have, if not the provisions of the New Covenant? And when Paul declared what the gospel is, namely that Christ died for our sins according to the Scripture, to what in the Scriptures is he referring, if not to those predictions which in fulfillment would result in the shedding of the blood of the New Covenant? How does it happen that the Gentiles got all of those things under Paul's ministry and we are being told today that Gentiles can have no part in them? What blood do these brethren claim for the forgiveness of their sins? The only blood that Christ shed was the blood of the New Covenant. Surely He did not come back later and shed some more blood which we could call the blood of the mystery. If a philanthropist should set up a huge fund for cancer treatment in one State, and then later on should designate that it be used for patients in all States of the Union, would cancer victims in those other States refuse aid on the basis that it was a fund for only one State? We would ask our extreme brethren to remember that the whole provision for our salvation was accomplished by Christ at Calvary in fulfillment of Scripture years before the Mystery was revealed to Paul.

We greatly err when we fail to distinguish between the *doctrinal* and the *dispensational* aspects of the New Covenant. In the very epistle where Paul tells us that Israel has fallen and is blinded, that reconciliation for the Gentile world has come in because of Israel's fall, and that the Gentiles have become partakers of Israel's spiritual blessings, he informs us that dispensationally the New Covenant is being held in abeyance and that it will yet be fulfilled upon Israel after that the fulness of the Gentiles is come in (Romans 11:26,27). But if anything at all is evident, it is that at this very same time Paul was ministering the great doctrinal truth of the New Covenant to Gentiles who were members of the Body of Christ.

Uses Earthly Elements

The third reason given why it is supposed to be wrong for us to celebrate the Lord's Supper is: *"It uses earthly elements."* We are supposed to be dead to the elements of the world (Col.2:20), to seek only those things which are above and not the material things of the earth. Now it seems to us that there is here a double confusion: a confusion of the words *earthly* and *worldly*, and also a confusing of the believer's standing and state. The word *world*, or cosmos, refers in the Bible to the evil world order or system. A worldly person is one who conforms to this present evil age. The word *earth*, on the other hand, refers to the physical earth, or planet, upon which we all live, whether we be spiritual or worldly. These same brethren who insist that the Lord's Supper is illegal for us because it makes use of earthly or physical elements, will discover, if they honestly reflect for a moment, that they constantly use physical elements in their spiritual service. The Bible that they use is printed upon earthly elements; the buildings in which they meet are made of earthly elements; their writings and lessons are sent out on earthly elements; their bodies in which they serve the Lord are made of earthly elements--in fact everything they do in some way makes use of earthly elements. Why is it that the Lord's Supper is singled out as an unlawful use of earthly elements? Why do not these brethren show a little consistency and stop making use of earthly elements altogether?

It is true that Paul warns us against carnal ordinances, but it is just as evident that the Lord's Supper is not a carnal ordinance; for he would not in one book advocate the Lord's Supper and in another written at the same period condemn such observance. Paul does not condemn carnal ordinances because they use physical elements, but because they denote an unfinished work. Even the Hebrew epistle, written to show the relationship of Israel to the New Covenant, plainly shows that one of the differences between the Old and the New Covenants was that the former was concerned only with carnal ordinances (Heb. 9:10), whereas the latter is not. Far from being a carnal ordinance, the Lord's Supper is the commemoration of a completely finished work.

We make the doctrine of the Scriptures ridiculous if we fail to distinguish between our standing and our state. It is true that our standing before God is perfect; it is heavenly; it is entirely spiritual. But what of our state? At the best it is imperfect, often sinful; it is earthly; it concerns much that is physical and material.

Other Ultra-views

The writings of others who teach that it is error to observe the Lord's Supper in this dispensation have been examined and further reasons have been proposed. Some Bible teachers claim that while it is true that the Body of Christ began historically with Paul before he wrote his first epistle (and that is what we believe), there was during the latter half of the Acts period a two-fold order, one for Jews and one for Gentiles, and that the Gentiles at that time were said to be the children of Abraham and were instructed to keep the Lord's Supper. But at the end of Acts, we are told, these Gentiles ceased to be Abraham's children; their relationship to the New Covenant was severed, and therefore they had no right to continue with the Lord's Supper. Now if this be so, we would surely expect to find some reference to so great a change in the later writings of Paul. But do we? There is not a word in the prison epistles stating that Gentile members of the Body of Christ no longer have any relationship to the blood of the New Covenant, or that being in Christ they are no longer Abraham's children as they were in Galatians, or that they are no longer to observe the Lord's Supper. When it comes to a subject such as baptism we have much written in both the pre-prison and the prison epistles which indicates the change and shows that there is for us but one baptism. But there is not the slightest hint of any change in regard to the Lord's Supper.

Another reason that has been given is that the Revised Version states in 1 Cor.11:20: *"When therefore ye assemble yourselves together, it is not possible to eat the Lord's Supper,"* and therefore since it was impossible

54

for the Corinthians to eat the Lord's Supper it must be impossible for us to eat it. This, of course, shows a very superficial type of reasoning. Paul does not state that it was impossible to eat the Lord's Supper, but that it was impossible for the Corinthians to do so in their divided and drunken condition. Had it been impossible for anyone to eat it, why then would Christ have told Paul to instruct members of the Body of Christ to do so?

One further general reason might be mentioned for not observing the Supper, and that is that the Body of Christ did not begin until after Acts 28:28, and since the pre-prison epistles of Paul are not addressed to members of the Body, 1 Corinthians is not for our obedience, and since the Supper is not mentioned in the prison epistles it is evident that we have nothing to do with it. Of all of the theories which have been propounded, this one displays the shallowest of reasoning. The very letter in which Paul gives instructions for the observance of the Supper contains this statement: *"Now are ye the body of Christ, and members in particular"* (12:27). Of course, these teachers know full well that this verse is in 1 Corinthians, but because it invalidates their pet theory they have to try to explain away the plain statement of Paul by claiming that this was not "THE" Body of Christ, but only "A" body. They make much over the fact that the definite article does not appear here, so it must be "A" body. Dr. Bullinger, who taught no Lord's Supper for today, was at least honest enough to show why no definite article was used by Paul. He stated in his Companion Bible: "There is no article because soma is the predicate." It is impossible for us to understand how one can really be sincere in handling the Word of God who teaches that the Corinthians were not members of the Body of Christ, when practically a whole chapter in the epistle is devoted to showing the fact that they were members and how they became members of that Body.

Lord's Supper Is for Us Today

We fail to see anything in connection with the Scriptural observance of the Lord's Supper which is in any way contrary to the dispensation of the grace of God. Of course, if we interpret the Supper according to traditional denominationalism, making it to be a means of grace whereby we receive the remission of sins, or a sacrament which changes the elements into the actual body and blood of Christ, then we would have to give up the practice or give up the grace of God. But we do not have to do either. We have merely to forget the traditions of the church fathers and

55

cleave to the simple instructions of the Word. In so doing we discover the following facts:

1. The Supper was a specific part of the commission of Paul for the Gentiles.

2. There is no set time or particular manner or ritual connected with it. It is simply, *"As oft as ye do this."*

3. There is no magical transformation of elements, no idea of a sacramental means of grace, and no meritorious work connected with its observance.

4. It is done for one reason: "This do ye in remembrance of Me."

5. There is no promise of visions, ecstatic experiences, or other emotional reactions. (This is mentioned because some people have argued that the Supper must not be for today because they never did have any particular emotional experience in partaking of it.)

6. It is to be observed *"till He come."* It is very evident that it will not be observed after He comes. If there is no place for its observance today, then there never was nor ever will be a place for its observance.

7. It has a very special relationship to "Body Truth"; for in 1 Cor. 10 Paul says to members of the Body of Christ: *"The cup of blessing which we bless, is it not the communion of the blood of Christ? The bread which we break, is it not the communion of the body of Christ? For we being many are one loaf and one body; for we are all partakers of that one bread."* Failure to discern this fact was largely responsible for the "partaking unworthily" by the Corinthians. Paul taught that our partaking of the one loaf signified that we are members of one body. Therefore if a man fails to discern the body (see any good revised version on 1 Cor. 11:29), he eats and drinks condemnation to himself. This is exactly what the Corinthians were doing. They failed to discern the fact that they were all members of one body. The rich fared sumptuously, even to the extent of banqueting and drunkenness, while the poor were neglected and were left hungry. This was an insult to Body truth and made a mockery of the death of Christ. Little wonder then that the Lord showed His displeasure by chastening these people. The bread and the wine were but symbols of the body and blood of Christ, but we can dishonor Christ just as effectively by misusing these symbols as we can dishonor our nation by trampling in the mud our star-spangled banner, which is the symbol of all that is dear to us as Americans.

BAPTISM

"ALL SAVED persons have been made members of the Body of Christ by one divine baptism (1 Cor.12:13). By that one baptism every member of the Body of Christ is identified with Christ in His death, burial, and resurrection."

Thus far practically all sound, fundamental believers would agree with our doctrinal statement on baptism. But most of these believers contend for two baptisms for members of the Body of Christ in this dispensation: Spirit baptism which makes us members of the Body of Christ, and water baptism, the purpose of which is a matter of considerable confusion and difference of opinion. Our doctrinal statement, however, continues: **"In the light of the statement concerning the one baptism in Ephesians 4:5, the statements concerning baptism in Colossians 2:12 and Romans 6:3, 4, and Paul's statement in 1 Corinthians 1:17 that 'Christ sent me not to baptize, but to preach the gospel,' we conclude that water baptism has no place in God's spiritual program for the Body of Christ in this Day of Grace."**

Since books have been written by men in the Grace Movement dealing quite exhaustively with the whole subject of Bible baptisms, it will be our purpose here, not to give an exposition of the more than one hundred passages in the Bible which touch on the subject, but rather to enlarge upon the statement quoted above.

Basic Facts about Baptism

There are several basic facts which one must understand before he can ever hope to grasp this doctrine intelligently. The first is that *baptism* is not a ceremony unique to the New Testament. Just because the word baptism does not occur in our English Old Testament, many have been led to believe that this is a brand new thing which God gave to the church in the New Testament, and that it would therefore be ridiculous to suppose that Christ would give this ordinance and then almost immediately rescind it. These same people can well understand how commands and laws and ordinances given to Israel through Moses have been rescinded in this present dispensation, but baptism--that is a new ordinance given by Christ to His church. The fact of the matter is that baptism is an Old Testament ordinance which was given to Israel through Moses, and was carried on

57

by John the Baptist and the Apostles, just as many other Mosaic practices were. Heb. 9:10 tells us that the Old Testament stood only in meats and drinks and divers washings (the Greek word here is baptisms), all of them carnal ordinances. Baptism was not an innovation to the Jews. Their divinely given religion was literally saturated with baptisms and to these added many more of their own inventing. When John came baptizing, the Jews did not ask what this strange, new ceremony signified. They knew what it meant, and so they asked: "*Why baptizest thou then, if thou be not that Christ, nor Elias, neither that prophet?*" And John answered them: "*that he [Christ] should be made manifest to Israel, therefore am I come baptizing with water.*" The only reason we do not find the word *baptism* many times in our English Old Testament is that baptism is the transliteration of a Greek word, and the Old Testament was written in Hebrew. The last word written to the Jews on this subject is found in Heb. 6:1, 2, where they are told to leave behind the elementary principles and to go on to full maturity, not laying again a foundation of the doctrine of baptisms.

Baptism Never an Arbitrary Observance

The next thing to grasp about this subject is that during the time that baptism was a part of God's religious program for His chosen people, it was by no means an arbitrary thing which one might or might not assent to. It was a definite command. Its practice was necessary to cleansing and forgiveness of sins, just as were the sacrifices and the shedding of blood. Even under Christ's ministry the people were told to bring their sacrifices and to do all that Moses had commanded, and of course this included baptism, as has been pointed out above. Today, many people who practice baptism say that it is nonessential, that it has nothing whatsoever to do with salvation or the forgiveness of sins. These people would do well to search their Bibles again to see whether they can find that kind of baptism therein. Such people know enough about the Pauline dispensation of the grace of God to know that no human religious works can have anything to do with our salvation today, but they continue to cling to a religious work, divesting it of its Scriptural meaning and inventing for it a meaning of their own. Others cling to this Old Testament ceremony, giving it its Scriptural meaning, making it essential to salvation, and thus deny the later revelation of justification entirely apart from the works of the law. For one who professes to believe in salvation by grace through faith apart from works, and who still practices baptism, it is suggested that he read again very carefully such scriptures as Mark 16:16, *"He that believeth and is baptized shall be saved,"* and Acts 2:38, *"Repent, and be baptized every one of you in the name of Jesus Christ for the remission of sins, and ye shall receive the gift of the Holy Spirit. "*

Figurative Use of Baptism

Another fact about baptism is that the word is used both literally and figuratively in the Scripture. As a matter of fact, of the twelve distinct kinds of baptism mentioned in the Bible, only five of them have any connection with the element of water. Very closely related to this aspect of the subject is the fact that baptism never means a burial. How foreign is the thought that when Christ baptized with the Holy Spirit He was burying people, or that when the Holy Spirit baptizes us into the Body of Christ, He is burying us in the church, or that when Christ will baptize in fire He will bury people in fire, or that when Israel was baptized into Moses they were buried in Moses, or that when the divers baptisms of the law were practiced the Jews were buried, or that when the Jews baptized their couches and utensils before eating they buried them, or that when John baptized Christ to fulfill all righteousness he buried Christ. Burial is completely foreign to the meaning or usage of baptism. And yet a great segment of Fundamentalism goes by the name of Baptist and claims that baptism means a burial, and since a burial is completely underground, one must be completely immersed in water in order to be baptized. Of course, they get this idea from Rom. 6:3-4 and Col. 2:12. But these passages do not say that we are buried in water, nor that baptism is a burial, but that we were buried with Christ through the baptism into death. We were also crucified with Christ, and raised with Christ, and ascended with Him and seated with Him. We have become so closely identified with Christ through the baptizing work of the Spirit that it can be said that when He was crucified, we were crucified; when He was buried, we were buried; when He was raised, we were raised. If we were buried WITH Christ, it must have been when and where He was buried. Christ was buried, not in water, but in a rock-hewn sepulchre. He was not put under an element in His burial, but His body was placed in a cave into which one might walk from ground level. The Scripture says that the believer was buried with Christ in Joseph's tomb. Surely there is not the slightest hint of a man-enacted ceremony in these great doctrinal passages. They speak of that stupendous work of the Spirit of God of placing us in Christ as members of His Body.

When baptism is used literally, that is, when water is used, there is always the idea of purification, cleansing and the forgiveness of sins. Surely all of the O.T. baptisms were for cleansing. The Jewish traditional baptisms before eating were surely purification ceremonies. John's baptism and that practiced by the Apostles at Pentecost was surely for the forgiveness of sins. When Paul was saved he was commanded to be baptized *washing away his sins.* And when John was baptizing at Aenon, a dispute arose between his disciples and the Jews, not about burial, but about purifying (John 3:25).

Paul Not Sent to Baptize

With these basic facts in mind about baptism, we are better prepared to examine the teachings of Paul for which we so earnestly contend. We believe that Paul's statement in 1 Cor. 1:17: *"Christ sent me not to baptize but to preach the Gospel,"* is proof that water baptism was not a part of Paul's distinctive commission from the risen Christ. Surely none of the Twelve could truthfully have said, *"Christ sent me not to baptize,"* regardless of what the local spiritual condition of the church might have been. But Paul did baptize some, just as he circumcised some, and observed other of the Mosaic customs. He did these things because they were still in God's program at the time he was saved, and he observed them along with the other Jewish believers. It was only after his ministry emerged from the Jewish to the great Gentile world that he made known that baptism was never an actual part of his commission.

Only One Baptism for Today

Everyone knows, of course, that during the book of Acts there were at least two, and perhaps three distinct baptisms. There was the water baptism practiced by the Twelve for the remission of sins; there was Christ baptizing with the Holy Spirit at Pentecost and in Acts 10; and there was the Holy Spirit baptizing into the Body of Christ. Yet in Eph. 4:5 Paul declares that there is but ONE baptism. What does this mean? Paul has quite a bit to say about a very important baptism, as has been pointed out above. The baptism of Rom. 6:3,4; Gal. 3:27; 1 Cor. 12:13; Col. 2:12 is a most important and basic truth of the Pauline revelation. He himself is the authority for the statement that water baptism was not a part of the revelation given to him. Therefore there is only one logical answer to the question: What is this one baptism of which he speaks? It surely is not water. We believe it is Spirit baptism through which we are identified with Christ as members of His Body. Strangely enough, a number of Baptists, as for example the late I. M. Haldeman, have seen the inconsistency of holding to two baptisms when Paul says there is just one for the church today, but they have been forced to take the opposite view, that Spirit baptism has passed away and that the only baptism left for the church is water. Since we cannot bring ourselves around to accepting the mathematically contradictory idea that two equals one, and since we cannot see our way clear in dispensing with the mighty baptizing work of the Spirit which is one of the chief characteristics of this dispensation and in its place holding on to a carryover from the law dispensation, and since Paul is so explicit in his statement that Christ sent him not to baptize, and since to Paul was committed the revelation of the mystery for this dispensation of the grace of God, and since among those who do practice baptism there is so much controversy and division, we are convinced that the one baptism which is so important in the keeping of the unity of the Spirit is the baptism by the Spirit.

Undoubtedly to the many who make water baptism the heart and center of Christianity it will seem that we have impoverished ourselves in giving up this practice. But we would ask, Does one make himself poor by giving up a check and taking gold in its place? Water baptism at the best was but a shadow of something far better. We have given up the shadow, but we have the reality. We have the Real Baptism.* Of course all truly saved people have this Real Baptism too, but many do not know it, and many dim its glory and never experience its power because they have substituted for it a human ceremony to which they are looking for spiritual blessing. We would with Paul make all men see what is this dispensation of the mystery, that all might know its power.

----
* See the author's book, *Real Baptism,* for a complete treatment of every reference to baptism in the New Testament.

61

THE LAST THINGS

THIS chapter in the exposition of our doctrinal statement will deal with the three articles which are eschatological in nature: Resurrection, Second Coming of Christ, and the State of the Unsaved Dead.

RESURRECTION

"Jesus Christ was resurrected bodily from the dead (Luke 24:39-43). Therefore (1 Cor. 15:21) all men will have a bodily resurrection (Acts 24:15): the saved to everlasting glory and the unsaved to everlasting punishment (John 5:29; Rev. 20:11-15)."

Since the next article deals with the various aspects of His coming, which are essential to a complete exposition of the subject of resurrection, we will quote that article also.

SECOND COMING OF CHRIST

"The rapture of the Church and the second coming of Christ will be premillennial. He will come first to receive the Church unto Himself (1 Thess. 4:13-18; Phil. 3:20,21) and then come to receive His Millennial Kingdom, over which He will reign (Zech. 14:4,9; Acts 1:10,11; Rev. 19:11-16; 20:4-6). Because of the nature of the Body of Christ, the resurrection and rapture of the Church, which is His Body, will take place before the Great Tribulation (Jer. 30:7; Matt. 24:15-31) at His appearing in the air (1 Thess. 4:13-18; Phil. 3:20, 21; Titus 2:13, 14; 1 Cor. 15:51-53). The resurrection of the other saved dead will occur after the Tribulation (Rev. 20:4-6)."

The real basis for hope in any dispensation is founded upon the resurrection of Jesus Christ. Paul's consistent testimony throughout the latter half of Acts is that the resurrection of Christ is the hope of Israel (Acts 28:20; 24:14-15; 26:6-8,23). In writing to members of the Body of Christ, he proves that apart from the resurrection of Christ we are all without hope (1 Cor. 15:12-19). Peter speaks of being begotten again unto a lively hope by the resurrection of Jesus Christ from the dead (1 Peter 1:3). Therefore sinful man, under the condemnation and penalty of death, is absolutely without hope apart from the resurrection of Christ, regardless of the dispensation in which he may have lived.

Two Phases of Second Coming

We believe that there are two distinct phases of Christ's coming. He will return first, according to 1 Thess. 4:13-18 and 1 Cor. 15:51,52, for members of the Body of Christ, and then later, after the Great Tribulation, He will come back to earth as King of kings to establish the Millennial kingdom. We oppose on the one hand the undispensational teaching of a general resurrection and general judgment of all of the saved and unsaved at the last day, and on the other hand we oppose the hyper-dispensational contention that the rapture of 1 Thess. 4:13-18 is not for members of the Body of Christ.

Bullinger Answered

When Dr. E. W. Bullinger changed over to the Acts 28 position, he wrote: *"We can quite understand, and fully sympathize with, those who like ourselves have spoken or written on 1 Thess. 4 as being the great charter of our hope of the Lord's coming. But we ought thankfully to relinquish it when we find we have a better hope; which we can enjoy all the more because we need not reproach ourselves with having robbed Israel of their hope . . . It may, after all, be the pattern of our hope, as presented later in Phil. 3:11,14 . . . The order of the two events may well be the very same" (Foundations of Dispensational Truth,* p. 112).

Many of those who have followed Bullinger's extreme dispensationalism, however, have gone over to the view of completely rejecting any idea of a rapture for the Body of Christ, and instead teach that the church of this dispensation will disappear from the earth by its members all dying. After the last member of the Body has died, then there will be the secret "out-resurrection" of Phil. 3:11, which will of course be unobserved by any one upon the earth. This is supposed to be something infinitely better than the rapture of 1 Thess. 4. It should be evident, according to this teaching, that no one living today could be absolutely sure that he is a member of the Body of Christ. The last member of the Body to be saved may already have been saved and may have recently died. The out-resurrection may already have taken place. We may after all be headed for the terrors of the Great Tribulation. As in so many other matters, here also extreme dispensationalism substitutes uncertainty and speculation for reality.

We believe that Paul holds out the same hope to believers in all of his epistles. The truth of the Lord's coming for members of the Body of Christ is clearly set forth in 1 Cor. 15:51 as *mystery truth*. The Colossians, after the end of Acts, were to continue in the hope which they had during the Acts period (Col.1:23). The Thessalonians were looking for the Lord from heaven (1 Thess. 1:10), during the book of Acts, and the Philippians were doing the same thing after the Acts in Phil. 3:20. Paul's statement to the Thessalonians,"*This we say unto you by the word of the Lord,*" is a plain inference that what he is talking about is a special revelation to him; for if he were merely reiterating what the prophets and Christ and the Twelve had been preaching all along there would have been no need to single this out as being the word of the Lord.

Rapture for Body Church Only

While it may not be a subject for dogmatizing, it would appear that only members of the Body of Christ will be raised and raptured when 1 Thess. 4 is fulfilled for being a mystery and having to do with a company of believers not foreseen by the prophetic Scriptures, it would logically follow that the prophesied resurrection of the just would be a different event from the unprophesied resurrection of the church. It is really upon this basis only that there is any evidence for a pre-tribulation rapture of the Body of Christ. That which is called the first resurrection, or the former of the two resurrections mentioned in Revelation, plainly takes place after the tribulation; for it specifically includes those who were martyred during the tribulation (Rev. 20:4). Many Premillenarians, denying the distinctiveness of the Pauline revelation, and hence denying the difference between the rapture and the first resurrection of Revelation, have gone over to the view that the church must go through the tribulation.

The hope that Paul holds out to all believers in all of his epistles is the coming of Christ out of heaven (Phil. 3:21) into the air (1 Thess. 4:17) to catch up to glory every member of the Body of Christ, whether dead or living. This coming of Christ is imminent, that is, it does not depend upon any fulfillment of prophecy before it occurs. It will take place before the tribulation. It is separate and distinct from the coming of Christ back to the earth, as predicted in the Old Testament and in the Gospel records and

64

in the book of Revelation. This latter coming of Christ will take place at the end of the great tribulation. Out of it will issue the judgment of the nations and the establishment of the Messianic kingdom, wherein all of the promises to Israel and to the nations through Israel will be fulfilled. This kingdom will not be the final state; for it will last only one thousand years, just half the time this present dispensation has lasted. It will be followed by the eternal state, which is described in the next article of our doctrinal statement.

STATE OF THE DEAD

"Nowhere does Scripture extend the hope of salvation to the unsaved dead but instead reveals that they will ever continue to exist in a state of conscious suffering (Luke 16:23-28; Rev. 14:11; 20:14, 15; Col. 3:6; Rom. 1:21-32; John 3:36; Phil. 3:19; 2 Thess. 1:9). The teachings of Universalism, of probation after death, of annihilation of the unsaved dead, and of the unconscious state of the dead, saved or unsaved (Luke 16:23-28; Phil. 1:23; 2 Cor. 5:6-8), are opposed by us as being thoroughly unscriptural and dangerous doctrines."

After the Millennial kingdom, when Satan shall have been loosed from the abyss, and shall have again deceived the nations, God will destroy the earth with fire. Then all of the unsaved dead (and all of the unsaved will be dead at that time) will be raised to stand in judgment before the great white throne. They will be condemned and then cast into the lake of fire which is the second death. God will then create new heavens and a new earth, wherein dwelleth righteousness. This will be the final state, as far as Scripture reveals--the unsaved in a conscious state of suffering in the second death, and the saved in a conscious state of bliss with the Lord in the new heavens and new earth.

Annihilationism Unscriptural

We oppose any theory that denies consciousness to man in the state of death, whether it be the first or the second death. Any such view leads directly to annihilation for the wicked, and in reality makes God's judgment of the wicked to be an exemption from enjoying the future. We believe that any ungodly sinner would be very happy with the prospect of being painlessly and mercifully put out of existence (as some advocates of this view represent it), rather than to suffer the woes of the second

65

death for ever and ever, as the Scripture plainly declares he shall.

Death is never presented in Scripture as a state of non-existence. We were once dead in trespasses and sins; yet we existed. She that liveth in pleasure is dead while she liveth; yet she exists. Lazarus was dead; yet he still existed. Christ died; yet He still existed. Moses died; yet he still existed; for he appeared on the Mount of Transfiguration. To be absent from the body is to be at home with the Lord. If the saved exist after death, so do the unsaved. The rich man surely existed after death. The man of sin is going to exist after death, for he is going to be cast into the lake of fire and be tormented day and night for the ages of the ages.

We likewise oppose any teaching of probation after death. There is no Scripture upon which such a doctrine can be based. It implies that man has not had a fair chance in this life. It gives reason for man to believe that he can cast off responsibility and live like the devil in this life, and then have a second chance, under far more favorable circumstances, to be saved in the life to come. God's Word is plain. It is appointed unto men once to die, and after this the judgment--not a second chance. Today--not in the life to come--is the day of salvation.

Universal Reconciliation Unscriptural

We are also unalterably opposed to the teachings of Universal Reconciliationism. We do not believe that God made the devil and forced man to sin, so that He is morally obligated to save Satan and his fallen angels as well as all mankind. The Concordant Version people believe and teach that after the second death and after the new heavens and the new earth (although the Bible nowhere describes the event), God will vivify all of the dead who have been out of existence for the ages, and that He will then reconcile all of these, along with Satan and his demons, so that all will finally be saved. To these people the judgment of the wicked in the lake of fire and the second death are analogous to a mother putting her child to bed early because it has been naughty, and then awakening it on the morrow to enjoy the full privilege of the household.

While these people speak much of grace and appeal no doubt to the natural mind with their presentation of God as one who will take the blame for everyone's sins (because He actually is to blame), in reality they make a mockery of grace. If God is in any way obligated to save man,

66

there can be no grace in His doing what He owes it to man to do.

We believe that God could have justly left all mankind forever in their lost condition without ever providing salvation for them. But we believe that through His infinite grace and mercy He has made a universal provision for man's salvation, but that the experiencing of that salvation is limited to those who believe the gospel.

MISSION AND COMMISSION

THE concluding article of our doctrinal statement has to do with the mission and the commission of the church.

MISSION

"The mission and commission of the Church, which is His Body, is to proclaim the message of reconciliation (2 Cor. 5:14-21) and endeavor to make all men see what is the Dispensation of the Mystery (Eph. 3:8, 9). In this, we should follow the Apostle Paul (1 Cor. 4:16; 11:1; Phil. 3:17; 1 Tim. 1:11-16). That distinctive message which the Apostle of the Gentiles (Rom. 11:13, 15:16) calls 'my gospel' (Rom. 2:16; 16:25) is also called the 'gospel of the grace of God' (Acts 20:24). We, like Paul, must preach the entire Word of God in the light of this Gospel (2 Tim. 4:2; Gal. 1:8, 9) and strive to reach those in the regions beyond where Christ is not yet named (Rom. 15:20; 2 Cor. 10:16)."

Our statement on this point of doctrine may seem strange to many Christians, as it contains no reference to the so-called "Great Commission" found at the conclusion of both Matthew's and Mark's Gospels. We do not believe that these accounts give us the commission for the Body of Christ. We do believe, however, that our commission has this in common with the so-called Great Commission: it is worldwide in character, and it is worldwide in a sense that the Matthew and Mark commissions could never be. It is significant, in this respect, that the first united effort in our "Grace Movement" was the organization of a missionary society which was named "Worldwide Grace Testimony," which fact in itself should be sufficient evidence that the commission which we follow is the same one which spurred the great apostle of the Gentiles to reach out to the regions beyond where Christ had not yet been named.

Great Commission Not for Us

There are a number of good reasons why we do not believe that the Matthew and Mark commissions are for us today. The first concerns the gospel itself; that is, the message of good news which God has given us to proclaim to a lost world. When Christ said to the Eleven: "*Go ye into all the world anal preach the gospel to every creature,*" He must have

68

intended them to preach the only gospel that they had knowledge of, namely, the gospel of the kingdom. It is evident that they did not know anything about the gospel of the grace of God, which Christ in glory revealed to Paul a number of years later. It is very evident from a comparison of Luke 9:6 with Luke 18:31-34 that the Twelve were preaching what is called "the gospel" during the time when they were completely ignorant of the fact that Christ was going to die and rise again from the dead. There must have been a vast difference, therefore, between their message and ours today, as surely no one could preach the gospel for today without preaching Christ's death, burial and resurrection.

At the time the so-called Great Commission was given, however, the Eleven had learned the truth about Christ's death and resurrection, and Peter proclaimed it at Pentecost. But there was still this great difference between his message and ours: Peter preached only the fact of Christ's death and resurrection, and this fact was preached, not as the basis of a gospel or good news, but as the basis of guilt and condemnation: "*Him... ye have taken, and by wicked hands have crucified and slain.*" "*The God of Abraham, and of Isaac, and of Jacob, the God of our fathers, hath glorified His Son Jesus; whom ye delivered up, and denied him in the presence of Pilate, when he was determined to let him go. But ye denied the Holy One and the Just, and desired a murderer to be granted unto you: and killed the Prince of life, whom God hath raised from the dead; whereof we are witnesses.*" We preach Christ's death as good news; Peter preached it as sad news, and then went on to say that if Israel would repent of this crime God would forgive them and send Jesus back to fulfill the promises of establishing their glorious earthly kingdom. Peter's message was not: "*Christ died for our sins:*' but "*Repent and be baptized every one of you* for *the remission of sins.*"

Contains the Kingdom Gospel

Peter's sermon in Acts 3 makes it abundantly clear that he was preaching the gospel of the kingdom. Up to this time this is the only gospel that God had made known. It was the good news that God would send His Son back to the earth to bring about the restoration of all things which had been predicted by the prophets of old. While we know that God is going to do this some day, and that is surely good news, we must know that is not the gospel which God wants us to proclaim to lost men today. Yet it was the gospel which Christ commanded the Eleven to preach in the

69

so-called Great Commission.

Paul referred to Peter's message as the gospel of the circumcision. He called it this because it was a message based upon the promises which God had made to Abraham in the covenant of circumcision. Paul called his own message the gospel of the uncircumcision, because it had nothing to do with the covenant of circumcision. It went back beyond circumcision to Abram, an uncircumcised Gentile, who was justified by faith, apart from circumcision, law-keeping and baptism.

Requires Water Baptism

The next objection to applying the Great Commission to us today is that water baptism is definitely stated as a prerequisite to forgiveness of sins in that commission. *"He that believeth and is baptized, shall be saved."* *"Repent and be baptized every one of you in the name of Jesus Christ for the remission of sins . . ."* We have already pointed out the fact that repentance and water baptism were important factors in the gospel of the kingdom, or the gospel of the circumcision. We do not believe that Paul's gospel contained these features. This does not mean that Paul did not call men to repentance, for we know that he did (Acts 20:21). We all believe that faith in Jesus Christ involves a changing of the mind, but Israel as a nation was called to repent of the rejection and murder of her Messiah. The subject of water baptism and its relation to the gospel of the kingdom has been dealt with quite fully in a previous article of our doctrinal statement.

Inseparably Related to Signs

A further objection to applying this commission to us is the fact that it contains certain substantiating signs which since Acts 28 do not accompany the preaching of the gospel of grace. *"And these signs shall follow them that believe: In my name shall they cast out devils; they shall speak with new tongues; They shall take up serpents; and if they drink any deadly thing, it shall not hurt them; they shall lay hands on the sick, and they shall recover."* Multitudes of Pentecostal people today are trying to prove that they are preaching the kingdom gospel instead of the gospel of the grace of God. They claim to exorcise demons, speak with tongues and heal the sick, and occasionally we hear of claims of raising the dead. Anyone who carefully investigates these claims must surely be convinced

70

that the results are but a counterfeit of the signs wrought by those in apostolic times. Doubtless these signs which accompanied the preaching of the kingdom gospel were a foretaste of the powers of the Millennial age to come (Heb. 6:5). Their purpose was to prove that the apostles had a message of authority which was able to usher in the Millennial kingdom, which was able to bring about the radical changes in nature which would overcome disease and even death. But our gospel in this present dispensation carries no promise of the deliverance of the world from these universal evils. Instead we are plainly told by Paul that the whole creation is groaning and travailing in pain together until now, and not only the outward creation, *"but ourselves also, which have the firstfruits of the Spirit even we ourselves groan within ourselves, waiting for the adoption, that is, the redemption of our body"* (Rom. 8:18-25).

Based upon Israel's Priority

Besides these three basic objections, the fact that the gospel of the Great Commission is the kingdom gospel, that it requires water baptism and special repentance as a requisite in the forgiveness of sins, and that it is accompanied with signs which point to the establishment of the Messianic kingdom here on earth, there is this further fact which we alluded to in the second paragraph of this chapter. This Great Commission was worldwide in character, but it must be recognized that it was not worldwide in the sense that all mankind was to be treated without distinction. In the kingdom gospel Israel as a nation is to have the ascendancy over the other nations. That is why the gospel went only to Israel during the time that Christ was on earth. That is why Christ told the Twelve to begin at Jerusalem and to evangelize Judea and Samaria before going to the Gentiles. Israel has a priority over the other nations in the Great Commission gospel. But in Paul's gospel for today there is no such distinction. It is plainly stated in his message: *"There is no difference between the Jew and the Greek."* Paul's gospel is *"made known to all nations for the obedience of faith."* The commission of the Body of Christ is truly worldwide without distinction in a sense that the kingdom gospel was not.

It is only natural that one who follows Paul must be missionary minded, for Paul was the greatest missionary that ever lived. He must be evangelistic; for Paul was not only the human instrument through whom Christ revealed His gospel of grace, but he was the greatest evangelist

71

who ever lived. He must be one who has given himself to selfless and tireless service, for Paul was also a living example of this beyond all others. And he must be one with a great heart of love for his Savior and for his fellowman, for Paul disclaimed that he himself was living. For him to live was Christ, and he became all things to all men that by all means he might save some.

The church of this dispensation and of this particular time needs to awaken to the fact that its commission is clearly set forth in the Pauline Scriptures. "God bath committed to us the word of reconciliation. Now then we are ambassadors for Christ, as though God did beseech you by us; we pray you in Christ's stead, be ye reconciled to God." We only frustrate the purposes and the work of God when we try to carry out the so-called Great Commission. We lose nothing of our evangelistic fervor, of our missionary vision, or of our love for souls by following Paul and leaving the kingdom commission for the kingdom as God intended it. We lose nothing--save the confusion and counterfeits which are so prevalent today; we gain everything.